History for Kids:
Ancient Egypt

Contents

Introduction

For the people of the Roman Empire, the Egyptian pyramids at Giza were older than the Romans are from our perspective today. This simple truth is one rather underrated historical fact that accurately illustrates the glory and importance of ancient Egypt. Most people have seen a picture or heard of the Egyptian pyramids and have at least some notion of the ancient civilization that lived there all those millennia ago.

For thousands of years now, Egypt has mystified and intrigued people from all walks of life, ranging from archeologists and other experts to regular folks who just have a healthy curiosity. Something about the ancient megalithic structures the Egyptians left behind draws us in and piques our curiosity. The idea that these supposedly primitive people accomplished such impressive feats of engineering so long ago is a testament to human resolve and ingenuity.

However, the Sphinx, the pyramids, and other structures are far from being the only legacy left behind by the ancient Egyptians. We now know of the many other complexities of the ancient Egyptian civilization that are just as impressive.

These folks had a complex social structure, a well-developed language, sciences, important infrastructure, a justice system, and religion. All of these aspects of ancient Egyptian life and society are indicative of an advanced civilization that might have more in common with contemporary life than one would think at first.

Not only did ancient Egypt prosper and achieve greatness during its time, but this civilization also impacted the world that came after it in many ways. The imprint left behind by the Egyptians comes as no surprise since their history roughly spans a period of three-thousand years. Ancient Egypt lasted much longer than many other famous civilizations and empires. The history of ancient Egypt is so vast and important that the pursuit of knowledge about this civilization has spawned relevant scientific disciplines such as Egyptology.

To make it easier to study such a long period of history, historiographers have divided the history of ancient Egypt into distinct periods, starting with the unification of Lower and Upper Egypt somewhere around 3150 BC. This time is when recorded history began, giving way to the Early Dynastic Period of Egypt and all the other periods that followed, which we will explore in more detail throughout this book.

Like any other civilization, ancient Egypt certainly had its ups and downs, but its history was ultimately a story of growth and advancement for the most part. This book will shed light on that story and put many things about ancient Egypt in perspective by chronologically exploring the civilization's history as well as many aspects of society and life. In the end, you will have a better idea of how and why ancient Egypt prospered and how this majestic civilization shaped the world well beyond its region.

Chapter 1:
Prehistoric Egypt

Throughout history, habitation and communities of humans flourished wherever nature was kind and giving. For example, for tens of thousands of years, the river Nile in northeast Africa and has been a life-sustaining magnet for many types of people, even those who preferred hunting and gathering their food instead of growing it, sprouting civilization along its banks. Even these nomads would never venture too far away, as going out into the scorching deserts always meant certain death.

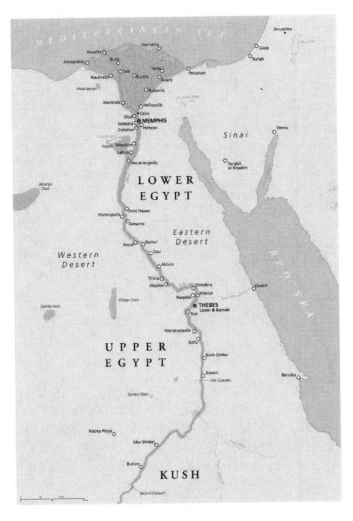

Ancient Egypt Map

Thanks to the periodic floods, the soil around the Nile was very fertile, so it blessed Egypt with both food and water. The ancient Egyptians later learned about irrigation, which allowed them to maintain their crops throughout the year. Just like today, the Nile was also an invaluable route of transportation of goods and people, which bolstered trade.

On top of the sustenance provided by the Nile, those barren deserts played their parts in making this location suitable for sustaining a civilization. Like mountain ranges and other natural obstacles, deserts are barriers that can make potential invaders rethink their courses of action. The Egyptians were getting rich thanks to the river and also enjoyed a certain level of protection thanks to the deserts around their habitat.

The period before the formation of dynastic ancient Egypt and the consolidation of the state is generally viewed as Egyptian prehistory and referred to as the Predynastic Period, stretching from between 6000 and 5000 BC to the unification around 3150 BC. Unfortunately, records and archeological evidence of this period are fairly scarce, so our knowledge of that timespan is somewhat limited which is unfortunate because this was the period when the ancient Egyptian civilization was taking shape and turning into the society we study today. Still, we do have a decent idea of what was going on and how the Egyptians lived before coming together under their first dynasties.

We know that the necessary foundations of civilized society were set thousands of years before unification. Evidence suggests that a lot of the land was suitable for Egyptians to graze their cattle some 8000 years BC. These times were the early beginnings of agriculture, which was still very primitive and limited. The hunter-gatherer people in the area were still largely nomadic, and the river Nile served more as a place to rest and get water than a place to inhabit.

Over time, however, these ancient people began seeing the benefits of living closer to the river and trying to create their own food sources. Around 6000 BC, agriculture began to develop, and these folks settled down and engaged in certain aspects of civilized societies, such as burying their dead and building tombs.

A few centuries later, semblances of industry (faience workshops) appeared in the ancient city of Abydos, which is one of the oldest cities in ancient Egypt and later became the capital of Upper Egypt. The remains of this city are located fewer than seven miles west of the Nile, south of the present-day city of Sohag.

Originating from Ur and Babylon in ancient Mesopotamia (a region spanning over the rivers Euphrates and Tigris across the Middle East), faience is a substance resembling glass or ceramic. Usually made from quartz or sand that was ground together with other substances like calcium or magnesium, the resulting material could be molded and shaped as the artisan saw fit and then heated to harden. This art quickly became an important aspect of early Egyptian culture.

The Egyptians used faience to make various figurines, amulets, and other items that were often used for religious and ceremonial purposes. With its bright, often bluish colors, faience resembles a precious gem if processed in a certain way and was also used to adorn clothing, pottery, and jewelry. Many invaluable archeological treasures, such as the well-known blue hippo known as "William," are preserved as Egyptian legacy. Many other well-preserved thousands of years old pieces adorn museums throughout the world.

Faience beads

Overall, these people were agrarian and had no writing system, which is why there are no written records. Written records came between 3400 and 3200 BC when the famous Egyptian hieroglyphs were invented. Prior to that, the story we know today is based on archeological findings such as the aforementioned faience, but also tombs and other things the ancient Egyptians started building during that time.

Agriculture and fine crafts of this later era aside, people in the ancient Egyptian lands before the designated Predynastic Period left their traces as well. In fact, some of those traces are so old that some archeologists have postulated that humans might have been converging in the Nile valley and beyond as far back as 700,000 years ago, although earliest crude structures in the form of shelters are estimated to be a bit over 40,000 years old.

Archeologists have identified and named quite a few distinct cultures that emerged from the tribes of these hunter-gatherers. Around 30,000 years BC, a group now referred to as the Halfan Culture emerged and prospered thanks to ever-improving stone tools. Archeological studies suggest that subsequent cultures such as the Qadan and Sebilian were most likely branches of the Halfan, emerging around 10,000 BC. These cultures were the foundation of agrarian, stationary settlements that would emerge later.

Scientists have long studied the transition of these people from their dynamic life of hunting and gathering to farming and settlement, and the subject still holds many mysteries. One area of particular interest is the Faiyum Oasis, which is an area just southwest of the capital Cairo and not far from the Giza plateau. This locale is where the first agrarian, settled culture formed in the period between 9000 and 6000 BC. Not only did people on this land continue to hunt and begin to use the fertile land for growing food but they also had a nearby lake for fishing and fulfilling their water needs.

The Cultures of Upper and Lower Egypt

What does the distinction between Lower and Upper Egypt mean? Although many people assume that Upper Egypt was to the north and Lower to the south, it was actually the other way around. These areas got their name from where they were located in relation to the flow of the Nile. As the Nile flows into the Mediterranean, the down-stream Lower Egypt encompassed the northern portion of the river, including its delta. Upstream from there and to the south lay Upper Egypt.

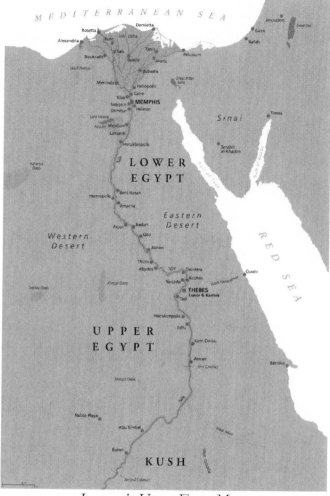

Lower & Upper Egypt Map

Lower Egypt

The development of the agrarian cultures occurred earlier and more rapidly in Lower Egypt. The culture that developed in and around the Faiyum Oasis is generally referred to as the Faiyum A Culture. This culture was crucial because it set many standards and foundations inherited and built upon by the communities that developed from Faiyum A.

And communities they certainly were, because this is where we begin to see semblances of governance and more organized hierarchy. Namely, forms of tribal government began to take shape and center around chieftains. Some of the tribes adopted a system of hereditary rule, where the chieftain position would be passed down through generations.

Dwellings usually consisted of huts built out of reed, but the people in the Faiyum Oasis also built underground storages to preserve their food supplies, which were usually grain. These folks also domesticated important animals such as cattle, goats, and sheep. Grain and other supplies were kept and transported in baskets and various pieces of pottery that Faiyum A developed.

Deserted reed huts in Sinai, Egypt

Archeologists identified a new culture, called the Merimde, emerging after 5000 BC thanks to all of these breakthroughs. These people have been connected to the western portion of the Nile Delta and, like most other ancient Egyptian cultures, they got their name from the archeological site where they were identified. This culture saw significant improvements in dwellings, storage, and settlement layouts. Such improvements went even further when the El-Omari Culture emerged around 4000 BC. Huts became much better and stronger thanks to the use of mud, but things like floor mats also made them more comfortable. The El-Omari ceramic evolved from what was available before, and they also had better tools thanks to the blades they invented.

During that time, other cultures started to develop simultaneously, such as the Tasian and Ma'adi. Buildings were no longer mere huts and shelters, but actual structures. The ancient Egyptians began to incorporate basements, hearths, stairs, and other improvements into their dwellings. On top of that, the way people approached the task of burying their dead also began to change with cemeteries becoming more commonplace.

Upper Egypt

The Badarian Culture was the first to emerge in Upper Egypt after 4500 BC, as well as among the first to make use of agriculture and other breakthroughs that already propelled Lower Egypt forward by this time. In many regards, this culture was very advanced that some archeologists believe was well ahead of their cousins in Lower Egypt.

On top of using huts in their settlements, the Badarian people also used mobile shelters or homes in the form of tents. Farming wheat and various kinds of herbs played a major role in Badarian life, while hunting was usually just a way to supplement the food supply. Possibly, the diet of the Badarian Culture was mostly vegetarian. Animals were used extensively for their leather or wool, which were important for the building of tents and clothing items. Despite their strong emphasis on farming, the Badarian Culture still produced a wide array of weapons that were useful for hunting but also defense.

The changes in the ceremonies and practices of burial in this period are especially interesting and important. The people of the Badarian Culture would bury their dead along with their cherished personal belongings and food. The idea that the dead needed these material possessions in their graves revolved around the belief that the deceased would use them in the afterlife. This concept would later become even more prominent and play a major role in the culture and religious practices of the ancient Egyptians.

The following period between 4000 and 3500 BC, often referred to as the Amratian Period, gave way to the birth of the Naqada I culture. Housing, tools, ceramics, and other important aspects of progress all continued to develop. The ancient Egyptians were now also giving growing amounts of attention to art and various fine crafts. The people made sculptures and figurines, but they also started putting more care into their pottery, ornately decorating the art with various motifs from daily life.

Toward the end of the period, previous burial traditions were developed further while still revolving around the same basic practices, particularly the burial of valued items along with the dead. However, the people were also starting to engage in the now famous art of mummification for their dead.

Ancient Egypt mummy mural

Archeologists distinguish the next 300 years as the Gerzean Period, which saw the rise of Naqada II. Apart from continuing to improve all the technological and social aspects of their culture, the people during Naqada II also made another crucial step, which was their greater focus on trade. Thanks to the Nile, these Egyptians could trade not only with other communities in their lands, but they also established contacts with the people beyond, such as in present-day Palestine. As always, trade facilitated development and growth in many aspects of society ranging from technology to art.

Other aspects of early civilization also emerged around this time. The sophistication of housing was at an all-time high, and huts gave way to homes with windows and made out of primitive brick, but brick nonetheless. Those who could afford it incorporated courtyards around their homes.

Model of ancient Egyptian house

The ancient Egyptians were already making use of rare metals like gold and silver at this point, so wealth became a concept, which was apparent during funerals since the more affluent people now had ornamented graves to show their status in life even after death.

Cemeteries became increasingly important and intricate as well. One of the ancient cities, Abydos, became one of the biggest burial sites where ancient Egyptians started building sophisticated, large tombs. Soon enough, locations like this became the first Egyptian necropolises, also known as the cities of the dead. The importance of these sites only grew over the coming centuries, and the Egyptians made them more elaborate over time. Abydos was definitely no longer a mere cemetery used by the locals, as archeologists believe that people from more distant lands would transport their dead to be buried there as well.

Abydos was far from being the only important center, though. Cities began to form, and some have already existed for quite a long time by this point, such as Nekhen, on the Nile delta. Other important centers included Naqada, Thinis, and others. These cities were thriving centers, started taking the shape of city-states, and engaged in trade with one another but also with cultures beyond, such as those in Mesopotamia. The ancient city of Nekhen was essentially the capital of Upper Egypt during this time leading up to the Egyptian unification.

Between 3200 and 3150 BC, the Naqada culture was in its final state as Naqada III. Archeologists have determined that the early Egyptian writing systems, known as the famous hieroglyphs, were developed prior to 3200 BC, although they were still very primitive and limited. The recorded history of Egypt started around this time. The writing was primitive in that there were no actual sentences, those would come some centuries later, although the Naqada III culture did continue to develop their hieroglyphs.

Egypt: Heiroglyphs

During this time, the influence from Mesopotamia was stronger than ever thanks to constant trade, and this showed in many ways. The ancient Egyptians imported new methods of construction for their buildings but also drew artistic influence. That effect has been observed in the symbols the Egyptians used in their tombs as well as pottery during this time. Apart from the material side of things, the Egyptians adopted certain beliefs and values from Mesopotamia, and this reflected on their religion. Another important step was the emergence of Egyptian colonies in some of the lands with which they engaged in trade, notably in present-day Israel.

All of these novelties helped Egyptian communities throughout Upper and Lower Egypt grow rapidly and their cities started getting bigger and bigger. In Upper Egypt, the most prominent city-states to emerge were Thinis, Nekhen, and Naqada.

Chapter 2:
The Unification and Birth of Dynastic Egypt

These former small communities were now important economic and political centers engaged in trade and other interactions with other locations. Of course, conflicting interests and the scramble for resources in some places soon led to conflict between the city-states. We don't have the clearest picture of how these wars went and exactly who led them, but evidence has provided enough insight for archeologists to develop a general idea.

Most likely, the city-state of Thinis ultimately took over Naqada and Nekhen. Who led these states and commanded their forces is something that's still debated. Some scholars named the last three kings of the Naqada III or Predynastic Period Scorpion I, Scorpion II, and Ka. Regardless of the conflicts, the well-developed urban centers throughout Upper and Lower Egypt were now more connected than ever and engaged in all manner of communication and diplomacy.

Overall, Upper and Lower Egypt began to take shape as actual kingdoms. If we were to impose contemporary concepts of borders and territory on these crude and early Egyptian states, they would look like two bordering states that are both fairly elongated and correspond to the shape of the Nile.

With the end of the Naqada III period, the dynastic era of the famed ancient Egyptian civilization was knocking on the door. The exact beginnings of the era of dynasties are fairly murky, and they are constantly debated on a couple of key points. Most of what we know comes from two major sources which are archeological evidence and something called *Aegyptiaca*, or *History of Egypt*.

This priceless document was written by Manetho, an ancient historian in the 3rd century BC, who put together an entire chronology of Egyptian rulers, starting around the time of unification. Despite its age and questionable accuracy, Manetho's chronology is one of the best pieces of evidence we have and is often cited by historians, archeologists, and other Egyptologists.

According to Manetho's chronology, a ruler known as Menes conquered Lower Egypt, built the capital city of Memphis, united the country, and established the first true dynasty of ancient Egypt making Menes the first official ruler of ancient Egypt. However, Menes is referred to only in Manetho's chronology and the Turin King List, both of which are ancient and disputed on the subject of the first rulers.

Menes, Founder of Memphis in Egypt

Many archeologists actually refer to Narmer as the unifier and first ruler of Egypt. Unlike in the case of Menes, significant archeological discoveries have been made which corroborate both the existence and rule of Narmer. One major piece of evidence is the Narmer Palette. This two-foot slab dates back to around 3100 BC and contains certain inscriptions and engravings. The inscriptions depict the successful and glorious conquests of a king who has since been identified by archeologists as Narmer. Archeologists have found other bits of evidence of Narmer's existence and rule as well, such as his tomb and a year marker with his name on it.

Given all this information, different theories have emerged and clashed over the years. On the one hand, a debate exists whether it was Menes or Narmer who unified and established Egypt. On the other hand, however, some experts believe that they were the same person and that "Menes" was simply the way in which Manetho referred to him. Furthermore, some Egyptologists have also suggested that Menes was merely a title at the time and could have thus been used to refer to numerous rulers.

On top of all that, the manner in which Egypt was united was contested. Egyptologists across the board are confident that the Narmer Palette depicts king Narmer conquering Lower Egypt, but some have pointed out that this could have been little more than a glorification of events for the purpose of propaganda. These scholars have suggested that Egypt may have been united peacefully.

Either way, Egypt was unified around 3150 BC, and the fact that the realm now had access to resources of Upper Egypt to the south, as well as those to the north, meant that growth was assured. The Nile Delta in Lower Egypt was particularly valuable, as was the labor force and agriculture in the northern parts. The new ruler to establish the capital in Memphis, not far away from the delta for these reasons.

Early Dynastic Period

Although there have always been some variations and disagreements over the exact designation of each period of Egyptian history, people generally agree that the period between 3150 and 2613 BC is the Early Dynastic Period. This period saw the rule of three Egyptian dynasties.

Whatever the absolute facts of the period leading up to this point were, the ancient Egypt we know began as its own kingdom beginning the most important periods of the traditional Egyptian chronology. A 3000-year civilization was born out of the process we have covered up to this point, and things were only about to get fascinating.

Experts believe Narmer ruled roughly between 3150 and 3100 BC, and he managed to accomplish quite a lot during his reign. For one, Egypt expanded considerably during this time, particularly further upstream along the Nile, going southward and over the Nubian Desert. Expansion also most likely occurred to the northeast across the Sinai Peninsula and toward present-day Palestine and Israel. Trade was stronger than ever with folks in Mesopotamia as well as the people who lived in present-day Syria during that time.

Narmer also put an emphasis on constructing many new structures and bolstered Egypt's urbanization. The cities grew rapidly, but they never grew past their capacity and ability to sustain themselves. Evidence has pointed to Egyptians being well-adept at managing their resources and building successful urban centers within their means. On the other hand, many cities in Mesopotamia were significantly larger and more impressive than those in Egypt, but their glamour was short-lived. Many ended up deserted after they depleted their natural resources and succumbed to pollution. The Egyptians didn't have this problem. Their cities developed gradually but surely, lasting for thousands of years thanks to the methods of city building adopted in those early days. By the time Egypt fell to Rome, many Egyptians were living in cities that were ancient even at that time.

Some Egyptologists believe that Narmer's wife, Neithhotep, continued to rule alone after his death, but ultimately, Narmer was succeeded by his son Hor-Aha around 3100 BC. Following suit with earlier developments, Hor-Aha expanded Egypt further and focused on building stronger trade relations. One important mark of Hor-Aha's rule was his emphasis on religion and apparent great interesting the matters of the afterlife. As a result, the Egyptians during this time developed mastaba tombs, which were essentially the precursors of the pyramids. The Early Dynastic period was also when the Egyptians were increasingly attributing divine properties to their rulers.

The ancient mastaba (tomb) in Giza complex, Egypt

After Hor-Aha died, his son Djer took over the kingdom around 3050 BC. Djer followed in his father's footsteps on most matters and also had a son by the name of Djet, who was the next ruler from around 3000 BC onward. What's particularly interesting about Djet's rule is that his wife, Merneith, was the ruler of Egypt after he died. This succession was the first recorded time a woman would rule over Egypt, and it was far from the last.

Merneith's son, Den, would assume the throne ten years later and prove to be perhaps the greatest leader of the First Dynasty. Den's reign lasted half a century and brought military successes, economic growth, and overall prosperity. Unfortunately, the rule of the next two successors would prove less ideal. Despite the unity and stability of Den's reign, the country later saw rebellions and strife over the throne. Records seem to suggest that Hotepsekhemwy ultimately came out on top and founded the Second Dynasty around 2890 BC which lasted until about 2670 BC.

Egyptologists largely agree that once Hotepsekhemwy assumed the throne, Egypt stabilized once again, but only for a short while. In fact, most of the Second Dynasty era passed in unrest and strife, which severely impacted the documentation of history as well, leaving Egyptologists very little to work with. What we do know, however, is that an important step for Egypt occurred during the rule of Hotepsekhemwy's successor, Raneb. He was the first ruler to officially proclaim his connection to the gods, which solidified the ancient Egyptian idea of divine rule for millennia to come.

King Peribsen, one of the following rulers, later managed to stabilize the country and continue to develop the economy, religion, art, and other aspects of Egypt. Peribsen's son, Khasekhemwy, continued to strengthen the crown's hold on the country, and he managed to centralize Egypt once again. He built many monuments at Hierakonpolis and Abydos and he fathered Djoser, who became the ruler around 2670 and founded the Third Dynasty.

Djoser's rule was impactful, to say the least. One of his most important contributions was the construction of the first pyramid, often referred to as the Step Pyramid or simply Djoser's Pyramid. This structure was an improvement upon the First Dynasty's mud-brick mastaba tombs, and it was quite a marvel for its time. It was built at Saqqara, the necropolis in the vicinity of Memphis.

Step pyramid of Djoser. Desert. Saqqara. Egypt

Although the Step Pyramid is a far cry from the latter pyramids at Giza, it was a monumental step and set the standard for future pyramids, the quintessential symbol of Egyptian culture. This structure was so important that we even know the name of the designer, Imhotep.

Djoser built many other monuments and led military conquests in the Sinai Peninsula as well. He was followed by other rulers who also built pyramids, such as the Buried Pyramid and the Layer Pyramid. The Third Dynasty persisted until Sneferu ascended to the throne around 2613 BC and founded the Fourth Dynasty, which marked the beginning of the Old Kingdom. The Old Kingdom would be the first of three major periods, in addition to the Middle Kingdom and the New Kingdom. Egyptian chronology also includes three intermediate periods between the kingdoms, all of which we will cover as we proceed.

Sneferu's Bent Pyramid

Chapter 3: Old Kingdom

The crucial period of the Old Kingdom spanned from 2613 to 2181 BC, although different sources give slightly different estimates. This period was the time when the unified Egyptian kingdom was in full swing. The Old Kingdom was when the ancient Egyptians accomplished many of the feats that have given them eternal fame, such as the most renowned of the pyramids at Giza. This period is also called the Age of the Pyramids.

Sneferu's Fourth Dynasty exercised strong, centralized control over the country and ensured stability through the era, which allowed the Egyptians to focus so much energy on enormous construction projects. The era of the Old Kingdom came to a close with the end of the Sixth Dynasty. Something else that Sneferu did, which would later cause problems, was to connect his dynasty to the cult of the sun god, Ra. The pharaoh was simply associated with the god, but the divine ruler and the deity were more or less on equal footing. However, the cult around Ra started to become more powerful over time, and subsequent rulers slowly reduced the pharaoh's status to the son of Ra.

Carving of Ra, the sun god, on the Abu Simbel temple

The first and most impressive of the pyramids was built for the ruler Khufu somewhere between 2589 and 2566 BC. This ancient wonder is now commonly known as the Great Pyramid of Giza.

Pyramids of Giza, in Egypt

Next, pyramids were built for the subsequent rulers Khafre and Menkaure. The Great Sphinx (c. 2500 BC) is also another one of the marvels constructed during this period.

Full Sphynx Profile Pyramid Giza Egypt

The pyramids are still quite mysterious in many ways, although their purpose was most likely to serve as tombs for the pharaohs. How exactly they were built is an even greater mystery. Egyptologists speculate the pyramids were built with intensive slave labor, a theory that exists to this day, but many disagree since the evidence for this claim is slim. Even though ancient Egypt did have slavery, it's entirely possible and more likely that the pyramids and most other megalithic structures were built by employees of various skill levels. In fact, many archeologists have pointed out that these workers were well provided and cared for. The pyramids looked quite different during that time, nothing like the rough, rundown structures they are today. Covered with a white limestone façade, these structures were pristine works of art in their time and a true testament to the affluence and prosperity of Egypt.

The age of stability and building started to wane during the Fifth and Sixth Dynasties due to a number of factors. Possibly, the Egyptians, for once, miscalculated their capacities and the gargantuan construction projects depleted the wealth of the state. The priesthood around the sun god, Ra, grew ever stronger because of the greater authority and status it previously received. The priesthood thus challenged the absolute power and divinity of the pharaoh. On top of that, local nobles and lords grew increasingly ambitious and independent, eroding the reach of the central government in Memphis. The era of the Old Kingdom thus came to a rather chaotic end when the last ruler of the Sixth Dynasty, Pepi II, passed away around 2181 BC.

Religion

By this time, the religion of ancient Egypt was well developed and present in all walks of life from the lowest peasant classes to the rulers. This religion was long in the making, but what was it really about? What kind of ideas and worldly perceptions drove the beliefs of the Egyptians? The religion was shaped by many factors that mostly had to do with how Egyptians lived during that time. Most of the foundation of ancient Egypt's religion had already been laid down during the Early Dynastic Period.

One important concept that evolved from Egyptian beliefs in the Early Dynastic Period was that of ma'at, which means "harmony" or "balance." Ma'at was the core concept of the faith, a building block of sorts. The ancient Egyptians also had their story of creation from very early on, in which the god Atum played a central role. As the story goes, Atum found himself standing in formless chaos and disorder before time even began.

Atum, His Wife Iusaaset, and Sobek

44

In the midst of that chaos, Atum was the one who brought creation into existence, but he didn't do it alone. At his side was "heka," which could be translated as "magic." This primal, eternal force of life also had its personification called Heka. Thanks to the force of heka, the formless world was given meaning and sense, shaping all aspects of existence as we know it, from the rising and setting of the sun to the more trivial parts of life. Because of this, heka was also the force that made ma'at possible. The incarnation of ma'at was the goddess of the ostrich feather, an important deity that each new ruler had to pledge themselves to.

Painting of the Egyptian Goddess Maat and the God Horus

Ancient Egyptian views on life and death were heavily influenced by their relatively peaceful way of life. The Egyptians often enjoyed security and abundance thanks to their ingenuity, geographical location, and the generosity of the Nile. Motifs of war, suffering, sin, and other unpleasantness were far in the backseat when it came to religion, and life was more or less viewed as a pleasant thing. Egyptians also saw life merely as a single step in a journey that lasted forever, hence their focus on burying the dead with their possessions and even food. The sense of belonging and oneness with the universe was a major part of the philosophy. The idea of eternal life extended to other living creatures as well, and the whole concept played an integral part in Egyptian religious practice for millennia.

Another important religious aspect was the attribution of divinity to Egyptian rulers. The connection of the rulers to divinity had two main parts, one through Horus in life and the other through Osiris in death. Egyptian mythology suggests the god Osiris was married to his sister Isis, and they ruled the world as a royal couple before gifting the people with all the wonders of civilization.

Osiris and Isis

Osiris had a brother named Set who murdered him out of jealousy but to no avail, as Isis used her powers to reincarnate Osiris and have his son Horus. Horus would go on to rule over the world and defeat Set. Symbolically, the god Horus is essentially a divine embodiment of harmony, and so his victory over Set was a victory over chaos and darkness. Religious teaching, funeral rituals, and masterpieces of Egyptian art would often make reference to this myth for millennia. These old traditions were very well established and integrated into Egyptian society by the time the Old Kingdom rolled around.

First Intermediate Period

The fact that Pepi II had no heir to succeed him as the ruler left a huge vacuum of power, which only added fuel to the fire in the already destabilized kingdom. The First Intermediate Period was a time of strife and unrest lasting between 2181 and 2040 BC. Egypt frequently became fragmented into different regions ruled by various local power players in conflict with each other and the Memphis government. To make matters worse, Egypt was hit by a drought around the end of the Sixth Dynasty which produced a famine.

The First Intermediate Period can also be seen as a time of transition. Even though the Old Kingdom saw stability and prosperity, most of the benefits in wealth and power were concentrated around the ruler in Memphis. The chaotic nature of the First Intermediate Period led to a redistribution of that wealth and power, which isn't necessarily a negative outcome.

The Seventh and Eighth Dynasties continued to rule in Memphis, but they didn't rule much beyond their cities. The country was soon split into two kingdoms. The power in Lower Egypt resided in Herakleopolis while the city of Thebes ruled in Upper Egypt. The Ninth and Tenth Dynasties ultimately decided to move the capital to

Herakleopolis, where they proclaimed themselves as rightful rulers of all Egypt. However, the family ruling in Thebes grew rapidly in power and engaged in many wars against Herakleopolis, often making great gains and seizing many cities from them.

The time came to end the wars and move onward when the prince of Thebes, Mentuhotep II, struck the final blow and defeated the authority in Herakleopolis around 2055 BC. In the course of a few years, Mentuhotep II reunified Egypt once more and strengthened his hold on the country, ultimately bringing the transitional First Intermediate Period to an end and starting the Eleventh Dynasty.

Chapter4: Middle Kingdom

Lasting between 2040 and 1782 BC, the period of the Middle Kingdom of Egypt was a time of stabilization and prosperity. Mentuhotep II's Eleventh Dynasty already existed during the First Intermediate Period, and he was somewhere in the middle of its lineage. Since Mentuhotep II was the Theban ruler who reunified Egypt, the Middle Kingdom begins with him or, rather, around halfway into the Eleventh Dynasty.

When he took over, Mentuhotep II established the capital of the reunified kingdom in Thebes, and the city developed rapidly. Over time, Thebes would become the most opulent and powerful city in the country. Throughout the time of the Middle Kingdom, the period was marked by cooperation between the central ruler and his provincial noble leaders, also known as nomarchs. The system worked very well, and Egypt became incredibly prosperous during the Middle Kingdom. This period is also referred to as Egypt's Classical Age, partly due to all of the priceless pieces of art created during the time. The art and literature was unprecedented at the time, and it influenced Egypt for a long time after the Middle Kingdom.

The ruling class during the Middle Kingdom drew great inspiration from the kings of the Early Dynastic Period, and even Mentuhotep II was likened to the legendary unifier Menes. Nonetheless, the political and social structure was quite different owing to the First Intermediate Period. Despite the fact that the country was reunified and under control, the strife of the previous era left a deep impact. The nomarch retained a meaningful degree of autonomy, influence, and wealth. A cultural shift had occurred and it wasn't going anywhere, but that shift wasn't necessarily a bad thing.

Mentuhotep II and Tuthmosis III Mortuary Temples, Luxor, Egypt

Even though Egypt was now fairly decentralized when compared to the Old Kingdom, the pharaoh still exercised utmost authority. The difference was in the fact that the provinces could exercise a degree of control over their lands and show initiative. This system afforded a higher degree of social mobility to the Egyptians, as rising through the ranks of society and politics was much more achievable than before.

The rule of the Eleventh Dynasty didn't last very long into the Middle Kingdom. Their time ended with the last ruler, Mentuhotep IV when he was assassinated around 1991 BC, as some Egyptologists believe. Mentuhotep IV's vizier (high official) by the name of Amenemhat assumed the throne as Amenemhat I and established the Twelfth Dynasty.

Thanks in part to the stable system established and left behind by the Eleventh Dynasty, Egypt flourished and entered a golden era during the Twelfth Dynasty. Amenemhat I introduced some novelties into the system of royal succession as well. Namely, every successor would be a sort of co-pharaoh with the current ruler before actually assuming the throne. This strategy gave new regents valuable experience and skill in ruling, but it also ensured a smooth transition of power. The capital was also moved during the Twelfth Dynasty to It-towy, which was a city just south of Memphis. The opulent and well-developed Thebes still played a major role as an important religious center, though.

Amenemhat also developed infrastructure and built Egypt's first actual army, which played a crucial role both in foreign and domestic politics. Prior to the formation of this army, Egypt relied on its nomarchs to raise armies from their provinces and answer the call of the king, but the armies were directly subordinate to the nomarchs. A formal standing army answered directly to the pharaoh, which helped keep regional lords as well as the priesthood in check.

Foreign policy was also a very important aspect of the Twelfth Dynasty. Egypt's trade connections to Palestine, Syria, and many other places outside of Egypt were at an all-time high. Egypt now sought to solidify its territorial claims, particularly by colonizing and strengthening its hold in Nubia to the south. The succeeding rulers in this long-standing dynasty continued in more or less the same fashion.

The Egyptians also finalized a long-standing conflict with the Bedouins during this time. These people made their way into Egypt during the disarray of the First Intermediate Period and were invading Egyptian territories. Construction projects were another mark of the Middle

Kingdom, with many rulers erecting their own pyramids and contributing to the dozens of pyramids we have in Egypt today.

The end of the Twelfth Dynasty began to approach with Amenemhat IV who ruled until 1807 BC. Amenemhat IV had no heir, so the throne had to be taken over by Sobekneferu, who was most likely his wife. Unfortunately, Sobekneferu had no heirs either, and so the illustrious Twelfth Dynasty ended with her death around 1802 BC.

Second Intermediate Period

Most Egyptologists agree that the Second Intermediate Period began with the ascension of the Thirteenth Dynasty, as this dynasty was a far cry from the successes of the Twelfth. The year of 1782 BC is the start of this period because that was when the new dynasty moved its capital back to Thebes in Upper Egypt. This move weakened the pharaoh's hold on the northern parts of the country in Lower Egypt.

Some records suggest that the Fourteenth Dynasty existed at the same time as the Thirteenth and was a rival for the throne from its center in the ancient city of Xois to the north. The Thirteenth Dynasty was marred with problems in its succession and struggled to establish its authority, which is what drew interest from other ambitious houses. Other Egyptian noble families weren't the only ones paying attention to the growing disunity in the country, though.

The real problems would start with a mysterious community called the Hyksos, which settled in Egypt in the final years of the Twelfth Dynasty. Historians and archeologists know very little about the Hyksos, but they speculate that these people originated from somewhere to the northeast of Egypt, possibly Palestine or Syria.

The Hyksos first emerged in the city of Avaris, which was an important center of trade established by Amenemhat I in the northern parts of Egypt. Being a trade center, the city was well-connected to the countries in the northeast, which drew in immigrants. These immigrants played important roles in the trade between Egypt and the peoples of Levant, so their wealth grew rapidly.

With wealth comes influence, and so the Hyksos were exerting significant influence in the region in the course of the Thirteenth Dynasty. Therefore, the Hyksos were far from being a horde of invading tribes to be suppressed - they were rulers. In fact, the traditional Fifteenth Dynasty in Egyptian chronology was made up of Hyksos rulers.

The succession of dynasties and their respective periods of rule have proven difficult to determine accurately. In total, dynasties thirteen to seventeen most likely all existed simultaneously during the Second Intermediate Period, each in their respective seats of power. The Hyksos rulers expanded over time throughout Lower Egypt and became so powerful around 1720 BC that the native rulers as far as Thebes were forced to pay taxes to them. Despite being foreign, the Hyksos dynasty adopted as many facets of Egyptian tradition and way of rule as possible.

Although some latter Egyptian historians spoke and wrote of dark times, Hyksos terror, and brutal subjugation, the situation might have been quite different. Historian Manetho himself wrote about a peaceful takeover without any pillaging or warfare. This account does seem legitimate given the fact that the Thirteenth Dynasty simply packed up and left Lower Egypt for Thebes. This move left a vacuum that was probably not difficult for the Hyksos to fill.

Hieroglyph with Hyksos Prisoners

To make matters worse, the military frontier of fortifications and fortresses that the Twelfth Dynasty left in Nubia to the south were also neglected by the Thirteenth. Somehow, despite all this neglect and partition, Egypt was essentially at peace. The now powerful Nubians to the south, the Hyksos out of Avaris, and the native rulers in Thebes maintained relations and left each other more or less free to rule the regions.

By the time when the Seventeenth Dynasty took over in Thebes, relations began to deteriorate when the native Egyptians started to lead military incursions against the Hyksos around 1580 BC. Clashes and skirmishes escalated into war relatively fast when Kamose assumed the throne at Thebes and declared war on the Hyksos to reclaim what he saw as rightful Egyptian land.

Kamose's campaigns were successful, and the Hyksos center at Avaris was effectively destroyed. Not stopping there, Kamose led wars against all foreign rulers over a period of some three years, mounting success after success. After Kamose's son, Ahmose I, ascended to the throne, he finished the job and reunified Egypt once again around 1570 BC, ushering in a new era.

Chapter 5: New Kingdom

Emerging from the disarray of the Second Intermediate Period, the New Kingdom lasted between 1570 and 1069 BC. This was a special period for a number of factors. First of all, the New Kingdom was a time of successful expansion that ultimately saw Egypt becoming an empire that stretched well beyond its previous borders. Secondly, the information we have about the New Kingdom is significantly better than that of some of the other periods. Perhaps because of this information, the New Kingdom was when many of the most famous ancient Egyptian figures emerged.

Although it's common and acceptable to use the title of pharaoh to refer to ancient Egyptian rulers throughout the ages, the New Kingdom was when this title came into official use for the first time. The word originates from Greek, and it translates as "Great House." The abundance of information we have about the New Kingdom of Egypt is largely thanks to the fact that literacy was increasing during that time, which had a great impact on historical records.

Eighteenth Dynasty was the first one of the New Kingdom, established by Ahmose I when he came into power in 1570 BC. The period ended with the dissolution of the Twentieth Dynasty. The breakthroughs and novelties that occurred during the New Kingdom were incredible and numerous, including many important changes to Egyptian society and system.

After Ahmose I extinguished the last bits of Hyksos influence in Egypt and neutralized all their strongholds, he shifted his focus southward to finish off the Nubian Kingdom of Kush. Ahmose I was successful here as well and Egypt's control over Nubian lands was restored. The king didn't merely reclaim lands and sit on the throne either.

In fact, Ahmose I focused greatly on rebuilding all the cities and important temples throughout Egypt and returning them to their former glories. He surrounded himself with a trustworthy inner circle and established a firm, central foothold in Thebes. The foundations were thus laid down for what would become the world's first great empire.

Ahmose I was succeeded by Amenhotep I around 1541 BC, and he left an expanded and well-fortified kingdom to his successor. Egypt was now expanding across the Sinai Peninsula and well into Palestine and Syria, but, most importantly, the country was stable and prosperous. Amenhotep I stayed the course and did fairly well with what his father left behind. He didn't do much conquering, but his contributions to art and Egyptian religion were significant. The famous Egyptian *Book of the Dead* was finalized during Ahmose I's rule. This book is essentially a collection of spells meant to assist one's transition into the afterlife.

Book of the Dead

Ahmose I also established artist colonies such as Deir el-Medina and he helped build and improve many important temples.

Ancient ruins at the village of The Workers at Deir El-Medina

During the New Kingdom, Egyptians introduced new tomb concepts as well and constructed the Valley of the Kings close to Thebes.

Valley of the Kings

Almost all New Kingdom pharaohs, such as the famous Tutankhamun and Ramses III, were buried here. The latter's tomb was more of a mortuary temple and is fairly well-preserved to this day.

The conquests took off once Ahmose I was succeeded by Thutmose I around 1520 BC. An attempted rebellion in Nubia was crushed, and Egypt expanded even further south, but Thutmose I also expanded further in Palestine and Syria. Egypt fought quite a few wars during the New Kingdom, such as those against the Hittites and the Mitannians. Nonetheless, Thutmose I continued the crown's contributions to important monuments and temples, such as the Temple of Karnak.

Ancient ruins of Karnak temple in Egypt

In 1479 BC, Hatshepsut rose up to become queen in succession of Ahmose I, and she is remembered as one of the greatest rulers of the period. Her expeditions were successful, notably those to the far southwest, but her construction projects and contributions to Egypt's art were even more impressive. The Thebes Temple of Karnak was becoming a true marvel by this point, and Hatshepsut made sure she left her mark there as well, in addition to her many other projects. Some Egyptologists argue that her stepson and successor, Thutmose III, made great efforts to erase Hatshepsut's trace from history in an attempt to maintain the illusion that only men could be proper pharaohs to Egypt.

Obelisks of Thutmose I and Hatshepsut

Karnak Temple in Luxor, Egypt

Whether or not this was true, Thutmose III proved to be a glorious pharaoh who elevated the country as the Egyptian Empire. The military was improved significantly under his reign thanks to knowledge taken from the banished Hyksos. The famous Egyptian war chariots, fine bronze weapons, and sophisticated tactics were all introduced under Thutmose III. His many campaigns were a string of successes, and he subdued most of the surrounding nations. Thutmose III remains as one of the best-documented pharaohs and is remembered as perhaps the greatest military genius Egypt had known.

Statue of Thutmose III

Thutmose III was followed by a string of other successful pharaohs, some of whom excelled in military matters as well while others were recorded as being great diplomats and economists. Egypt reached a cultural peak around 1386 BC when Amenhotep III became pharaoh. The country was stable and prosperous, but semblances of problems appeared as the priesthood of the Cult of Amon-Ra became increasingly powerful and wealthy. The cult revolved around a fusion of the gods Amon and Ra, which occurred after the banishment of the Hyksos and reunification of Egypt.

Statue of Amenhotep III

The many contributions the pharaohs made to the cult's Temple of Karnak show us the importance ascribed to these priests, making them incredibly powerful over time. Toward the end of New Kingdom, the cult's temple alone employed tens of thousands of priests, some of whom became so powerful and affluent that they challenged the pharaoh.

Still, this time saw unprecedented prosperity and stability in Egypt. The country was vast, well-defended, and rich. People could afford to focus on many things that led to improvements in the overall quality of life. The Egyptians brewed beer, engaged in sports, and improved many other venues of leisure and enjoyment, such as baths. Important breakthroughs occurred in medicine, and the standards of health in the New Kingdom were impressive. The ancient Egyptians are known to have practiced effective surgery, studied gynecology, and made great innovations in the area of hygiene as well.

Things began to take a turn in 1353 BC when Amenhotep IV came into power and decided to suppress the influence of the priests. He introduced monotheism into Egyptian society which had been worshipping many gods for a long time. Amenhotep IV thus declared a new sun god by the name of Aten, banished all the previous deities, and changed his own name to Akhenaten to reflect his devotion. This move succeeded in taking power from the priests for a while, and Akhenaten also moved the capital to Amarna in Middle Egypt.

However, the project failed after his death, and Egyptians went back to their old way. His son, the famed Tutankhamun, made sure that his father's religious experiment was erased and the capital was moved back to Thebes. Tutankhamun is one of the most famous rulers of Egypt to this day, owing mostly to his well-preserved tomb and the iconic

Death Mask. Otherwise, his reign wasn't very long because he died prematurely.

Tutankhamun mask

The last ruler of the Eighteenth Dynasty was Horemheb. Because he had no heir, he had to appoint his vizier, Paramesse, as the successor. Once he took the throne in 1292 BC, Paramesse changed his name and became Ramesses I. This name would go down in history during the reign of Ramesses the Great (Ramesses II), who assumed the title of pharaoh in 1279.

*Colossus of The Great Temple of Ramesses II,
Abu Simbel, Egypt*

Ramesses II's exploits are legendary in all aspects of his rule. He is famous thanks to biblical references, the glorious Battle of Kadesh against the Hittites in 1274 BC, his countless monuments and temples such as the Abu Simbel temple, and much else. Thanks to Ramesses II's adeptness at both war and diplomacy, Egypt was also the first country ever to sign an official peace treaty in 1258 BC, known as the Treaty of Kadesh.

This pharaoh's legacy was so immense that he was known as the Great Ancestors to those who came after. His death, after an impressively long life of 96 years, was perceived as almost apocalyptic by many of his subjects in Egypt.

The Nineteenth Dynasty went on until the throne was usurped by Setnakhte in 1190 BC when he established the Twentieth Dynasty. Egypt's wealth and stability slowly declined, and they had long-standing problems with the so-called Sea Peoples who were constantly invading. The Sea Peoples weren't defeated until 1178 BC when Ramses III finally managed to subdue them.

Rameses III Painted Relief, Medinet Habu,
Theban Necropolis, Luxor, Egypt

Nonetheless, the empire was increasingly difficult to control. All the success and splendor of Ramses II's rule, despite its countless benefits, also ensured that certain folks became incredibly rich and powerful in the kingdom, especially those in the priesthood. The era of the New Kingdom was reaching its end toward 1077 BC under the rule of Ramesses XI. The rule of the pharaoh was outright defied by powerful local rulers and the country began to splinter and descend once more into disunity. The Twentieth Dynasty officially collapsed around 1069, starting the Third Intermediate Period.

Chapter 6: Decline and Final Conquests

Power in Egypt was already split before the Third Intermediate Period even began and, early in the period, Egypt was effectively ruled from two centers in Thebes and Tanis. As the power of the pharaoh diminished throughout the Twentieth Dynasty, the Amon priests only became hungrier and more powerful. Not only was the Cult richer than the pharaoh, but they effectively took over Thebes and made great efforts to deprive the pharaoh title of any true meaning and influence.

Up to this point, the pharaoh was the intermediary between the gods and the people, thus executing divine will. As the priesthood of Thebes became stronger, however, the priests began to consult Amon-Ra directly, which effectively made them rulers. The priestly authority at Thebes was a total theocracy where the will of the gods permeated all facets of society and the system. In accordance with that, the priesthood soon claimed sovereignty over the land in a bid to legitimize a new form of rule.

When Ramses XI died, the man who buried him, Smendes, became his successor as per Egyptian custom. At the time, Smendes governed the town of Tanis in Lower Egypt and moved the capital there when he established the Twenty-first Dynasty. His rule in Tanis was much more secular in nature than was the case in Thebes.

Things would never be the same in Egypt again, though. Local power players emerged and foreign rulers swooped in from Nubia to the south and Libya to the northwest. The foreigners soon entrenched their positions and affected Egypt for centuries to come. The Third Intermediate Period saw the rule of dynasties 21 through 25, two of which weren't even native Egyptian. The Kingdom of Kush from Nubia ultimately unified Egypt under its rule around 752 BC, and the country was developing. War was on the horizon, however, and the Assyrians started to aspire toward Egyptian lands. The Assyrian Empire captured and lost Egypt a couple of times by 656 BC.

Late Period

The Late Period of Egyptian civilization began in 525 BC with the Persian invasion of the kingdom after a perceived insult from the Egyptians. Namely, some accounts state that Egypt insulted the Persians by refusing to marry the pharaoh's daughter off to Cambyses II of Persia upon his request. The Persian armies moved in swiftly through the Nile Delta and struck at the city of Pelusium.

Initially, the Persians failed to break through the city walls, but they began to strategize. Namely, some Egyptologists believe that Cambyses II exploited the Egyptian love for cats. Cats were essentially holy in Egypt and hurting them was considered an outrage against the gods. Knowing this, the Persians collected all the stray cats they could find in the area and forced them ahead of their army, at which point the Egyptians surrendered rather than risk hurting the animals. Such was the account by famed Greek historian, Herodotus, at least.

Cambyses II, ruler of the Achaemenid Persians

After close to two centuries of rule by the Saite Dynasty, Egypt was subjugated to the Persians after Psammetichus III's defeat at Pelusium in 525 BC. In the beginning, the Persians granted Egypt autonomy in matters of religion and culture, and they adapted their rule over the country to be in keeping with Egyptian traditions. That didn't last, however, and Persian rule soon turned into tyranny under Xerxes between 486 and 465 BC. Uprisings followed and saw success around 404 BC, which marked the beginning of native dynasties 28 through 30.

Not too long after that, the Persians struck and seized Egypt once more in 343 BC. However, the Persians met their own match elsewhere, and Alexander the Great soon marched into Egypt peacefully and without resistance, being greeted as a liberator.

Hellenistic Period and Roman Conquest

The Late Period, which was the last of the major periods of ancient Egyptian history, ended with Alexander's conquest in 332-331 BC. The Hellenistic Period is a historical designation for the history of lands far beyond just Egypt, so it's not part of the official Egyptian chronology, although Egypt continued to exist during the era. To that effect, Egypt went through the Hellenistic period in the time between Alexander's conquest and the fall to the Roman Empire.

One of Alexander's first orders of business was to establish the city of Alexandria in the Egyptian port city of Rhakotis. This Mediterranean coastal city would grow and thrive through the ages to become the major urban center that is home to some five million people today. Alexander the Great didn't stick around too long after giving his instructions to the new administration. He went on about his conquests, and the new Macedonian administration proceeded to build up the city and engage in many other infrastructural projects throughout the Nile Delta.

A bust of Alexander The Great in central Alexandria, the city named after him.

The initial conquest and influence were only the beginning of Macedonian rule in Egypt, though. Alexander the Great met his end in 323 BC, and the rule of Egypt was passed off to his general

Ptolemy I Soter, who ruled the country between 323 and 285 BC.

Ptolemy I Soter

Ptolemy's rule marked the beginning of the Ptolemaic Dynasty, which lasted until 30 BC. During this Greek dynasty, Egyptian culture experienced a temporary revival and was held in high regard. The famous Lighthouse, or Pharos, of Alexandria was built during this time.

Lighthouse of Alexandria

Even though it came at such a late period of the Egyptian civilization, the Ptolemaic Dynasty produced some legendary leaders. Names like Cleopatra VII ring out to this day. Toward 30 BC, the Roman Empire was long in the making just across the Mediterranean. Cleopatra surrendered the country to Augustus in 31 BC, who promptly annexed the territory.

Cleopatra (After an Egyptian Representation)

Egypt's age and mystery seemed to enchant every conquering warrior and hero who came to the Nile. Through Persians, Greeks, and Romans, the Egyptian culture, traditions, religion, and everything else that made it unique was left mostly undisturbed. No violent attempts to suppress the ancient Egyptian civilization were ever undertaken in all those centuries. Conquest after conquest, the achievement of this ancient nation commanded respect and admiration from all who came, no matter how great they were.

The Roman rule went on for six centuries, however, and Egyptian identity waned over time as major social and cultural shifts took place throughout the whole region and the known world. Christianity became the official religion of the Egyptian Province of Rome, but that too came and passed by the 7th century AD when Arabs swooped in with Islam and conquered Egypt for good.

Chapter 7:
Legacy and Impact

The ancient Egyptians left us with more than just a few impressive mega structures to marvel at or some interesting hieroglyphic writings to decipher. This civilization left a significant mark on our world and impacted today's society in more ways than one. Some of the ancient Egyptian influences have been important contributions to mankind while others could be seen as far less monumental, but some of them might surprise you.

As a whole, the legacy of ancient Egypt is vast and deserves volumes of books to really do it justice. For instance, what these ancient people left behind has inspired countless works of art through the centuries. Monuments of this culture have also influenced architecture in many instances, some of which are famous. Since the beginning, monuments like obelisks were adopted and reimagined by other cultures such as the ancient Greeks. Even in the modern era, such designs play their part, one example being the Washington Monument.

The Washington Monument in Washington DC

On the other hand, the very existence of the remnants of ancient Egypt continues to affect the world in other, less tangible ways. The Giza plateau, to this day, is what draws in many tourists to Egypt, which is an important boost to the country's economy. Popular culture is also seemingly forever infatuated with ancient Egypt. That fascination has given rise to all sorts of interesting folks and ideas, ranging from those who like to speculate about what may still lay unfound to those who think that the pyramids were built by aliens from outer space. Be that as it may, reflecting on how Egypt's legacy has shaped the world is a good way to round off this fabulous story.

Bowling

Right off the bat, you might be surprised to find out that the ancient Egyptians were most likely the first people to invent bowling. Of course, the game was fairly different than how we know bowling today, but many of the base elements of the game were there. Namely, archeologists have discovered a grave that contained pins, although their use for bowling was just a theory by the researchers. Other discoveries, however, have shown that the ancient Egyptians also crafted balls and built lanes to roll them on. One of the discovered lanes has a hole in the middle, which suggests that the game, although similar to bowling, was not exactly focused on knocking down pins.

Mathematics

Far more important are the ancient Egyptian contributions to mathematics. Namely, the Egyptians probably were the first people to use geometry. Their geometry was so sophisticated that they had specialists, who were referred to as arpedonapti. One of the uses for geometry in ancient Egypt was to calculate and measure land. This innovation was just one of many that eventually made their way to Greece and significantly impacted society there. Not only that, but the ancient Egyptians were also well-adept at division and multiplication, and they also invented fractions. Essentially, many mathematical breakthroughs that occurred in ancient Egypt were unheard of throughout the world at the time, and for quite a while after that.

Papyrus Revolution

Old vintage scroll

Papyrus was a critical invention. At a time when engraving things into stone, wood, and other hard materials was commonplace, the invention of papyrus revolutionized writing. This light material was easy to carry, transport, and store, which made it so much more practical than stone tablets, for instance. The ancient Egyptians used papyrus and reed pens for thousands of years until the regions to their north and northeast caught on to this invention's usefulness. Over time, papyrus became one of Egypt's most sought-after products, so they exported it far and wide and made a lot of money from it.

Medicine and Surgery

Images of medical equipment

Although medicine was very primitive, of course, the ancient Egyptians used papyrus and their writing system to keep records of various diseases or injuries and their respective treatments. For that time, the idea of writing down these medical practices and sharing knowledge about it in written form was quite advanced. Another interesting aspect of ancient Egyptian medicine was its reliance on actual science as opposed to superstition. Instead of trying to spell health problems away or invoke the spirits, the ancient Egyptians used herbs and other physical remedies to treat sickness and injury. On top of that, the Egyptians were some of the world's first surgeons, and they had a variety of tools for the job.

Wigs

Ancient Egyptians, especially those from the upper echelons, cared about making themselves presentable, particularly in important settings. However, growing a beautiful head of hair was less than desirable due to the climate of their desert country and the scorching Sun. Wigs were thus invented so that people could have the best of both worlds. These wigs were made from real hair as well as other materials, and the trend of wearing them had practical benefits that went beyond just aesthetics. Apart from keeping people's heads cool, wigs helped reduce the spread of parasites such as lice, which could also carry disease. All in all, wigs were a very progressive and clever invention for such an ancient society.

Toothpaste

That's right; the ancient Egyptians even took steps to improve their dental hygiene and health with methods similar to our own. Many civilizations came up with their own mixtures and pastes for this purpose, but Egyptian toothpaste is still the oldest ever recorded. Of course, the ancient Egyptians also wrote down their recipe for the toothpaste so it's something that can be recreated, and it has been. The toothpaste was found to indeed have a positive effect on oral health, although it's not nearly as effective as what we have today. Furthermore, the Egyptians also crafted crude but efficient toothbrushes to go along with the paste.

Glass

We mentioned Egyptian faience early in this book, but that glassy material was being developed thousands of years before the time of the pharaohs. The ancient Egyptians went far beyond faience through the millennia, and the glass they were producing later on was very impressive for their time. The fine glass made by the Egyptians was used for all kinds of purposes, such as the crafting of beautiful and pristine vases and many types of ornamental items. The vases themselves were often works of art, but they had practical uses as well. Another impressive feat was the invention of red glass, which was very difficult to produce. Over time, Egyptian glass products were another major export and influence, and the country's craft ultimately made its way to the Romans.

Farming and Construction

Of course, perhaps the greatest aspects of ancient Egyptian legacy were their feats of engineering and construction. Structures like the pyramids are impressive enough on their own, but the ingenuity and the painstaking physical and mental work that went into them are just as awe-inspiring. In fact, the ancient Egyptians were almost undoubtedly the world's first true builders. Flooring, roofing, and refurbishing complemented the scale of their major construction projects. The ancient Egyptians invented indoor lighting, the concept of master bedrooms, cement, mortar, rope, scaffolding, mass-produced bricks, and so much more. They were the true pioneers of architecture and construction on all levels of scale.

These were but a few of the countless innovations introduced by the ancient Egyptians. We might not use papyrus or faience nowadays, but such inventions impacted other civilizations around Egypt and altered the course of history for centuries to come. Those other people then improved upon what they learned and they passed the knowledge further onward, allowing that knowledge, with all its improvements, to ultimately reach us today.

Conclusion

The whole story of ancient Egypt can hardly be compressed into a single book, and it requires volumes upon volumes of scientific resulting from decades of research. Even then, our understanding and knowledge are limited to the things we can learn from the often scarce clues and remnants preserved for us so graciously at the mercy of time.

Because of this, a lifetime of study and commitment is needed to grasp the whole picture and truly understand everything that the story of ancient Egypt has to offer. The author's hope is that this book has given you a valuable introduction into the mystifying, yet fascinating world of ancient Egypt and piqued your interest to learn more. For those who develop a genuine interest in the subject, there is no shortage of things to learn about the rich history of Egypt.

The ancient Egyptian civilization is also a testament and reminder of how unconditionally kind nature can be through the things she provides. The river Nile and the ideal conditions it offers along its bank showed us, through ancient Egypt and many times after, that even ancient people could accomplish incredible feats as long as they cherished the special relationship between nature and mankind.

In the end, ancient Egypt left us with accomplishments and lessons that will last through the ages and probably continue to fascinate us for as long as we occupy this planet. What's more, there is always a possibility that we might discover new findings and understand even more about the Egyptians. If some stones are still unturned, they are sure to be found in time by new generations of talented researchers with a thirst for knowledge. After all, that's how many of the renowned archeologists and other experts who gave us so much knowledge started their journey – as young people or even children who just wanted to know more.

More from Us

Made in the USA
San Bernardino, CA
08 August 2019

YOU CHOOSE
BOOKS™
Historical Eras

The Aztec Empire

An Interactive History Adventure

by Elizabeth Raum

Consultant:
Colin M. MacLachlan, PhD
History Department
Tulane University

CAPSTONE PRESS
a capstone imprint

You Choose Books are published by Capstone Press,
1710 Roe Crest Drive, North Mankato, Minnesota 56003
www.capstonepub.com

Library of Congress Cataloging-in-Publication Data
Raum, Elizabeth.
The Aztec Empire : an interactive history adventure / by Elizabeth Raum.
    p. cm. — (You choose books. Historical eras.)
Includes bibliographical references and index.
Summary: "Describes life during the Aztec Empire. The readers' choices reveal the historical
details of life as a worker, a warrior, and a European explorer"—Provided by publisher.
ISBN 978-1-4296-4779-3 (library binding)
ISBN 978-1-4296-9474-2 (paperback)
ISBN 978-1-62065-377-7 (ebook PDF)
1. Aztecs—Juvenile literature. I. Title.
F1219.73.R375 2013
972—dc23   2012002191

Editorial Credits
Kristen Mohn, editor; Bobbie Nuytten, designer; Wanda Winch, media researcher;
    Danielle Ceminsky, production specialist

Photo Credits
Alamy: dieKleinert, 46, North Wind Picture Archives, 6, 60, 70, Ruslan Bustamante, 100;
Art Resource, N.Y.: Werner Forman, 96; Bridgeman Art Library; National Geographic
Stock/H. Tom Hall, cover, Private Collection/Stephen Reid, 80; Capstone: Carl Lyons, 10,
68; Dreamstime: Czuber, 17; Getty Images: Bettmann, 38, 67, 88, National Geographic Stock:
Felipe Dávalos 52; Rourke Publishing, LLC: How They Lived: An Aztec Warrior, 40; www.
mexicolore.co.uk: 24, 28, Felipe Dávalos, 12, 32, Ian Mursell, 55

Printed in China.
001468

TABLE OF CONTENTS

ABOUT YOUR ADVENTURE

YOU are living on the island of Tenochtitlan in the Valley of Mexico around the 15th century. The Aztec people of the island are brave, creative, and intelligent. But European conquistadors are moving in. What will happen to the Aztecs and their way of life?

In this book you'll explore how the choices people made meant the difference between life and death. The events you'll experience happened to real people.

Chapter One sets the scene. Then you choose which path to read. Follow the directions at the bottom of each page. The choices you make will change your outcome. After you finish your path, go back and read the others for new perspectives and more adventures.

YOU CHOOSE the path
you take through history.

Tenochtitlan, the capital city of Aztec Mexico, was built on an island in the 1300s.

City of Dreams

The Aztec people founded one of the most powerful empires in history. The Aztecs, who were also called the Mexica, lived in Atzlan. Atzlan was located somewhere in northern Mexico or the southwestern United States. In about 1100, the Mexica left Atzlan and worked their way south for more than 200 years. They reached Mexico's Central Valley and settled on an island in Lake Texcoco in 1325. There they began building the great city of Tenochtitlan.

They built temples and pyramids in the city center. These buildings rose high above the streets and canals of the island. Stone serpent heads guarded the pyramids. Nearby were large villas that belonged to wealthy nobles. There were gardens, fountains, and even zoos.

Turn the page.

Aztec workers lived farther from the city center. Five or six adobe huts shared a courtyard where people cooked and visited. Neighborhoods were organized by jobs.

Carpenters lived in one neighborhood. Potters and basket makers lived in others. Farmers planted crops and flowers along the shoreline or on man-made islands called chinampas. Aztec traders kept the city supplied with goods of all kinds.

The Aztecs fought wars nearly all the time. They captured nearby cities and towns, not to destroy them, but to claim their riches. Captured towns had to pay tributes to Tenochtitlan. These tributes might be crops, cloth, or precious metals such as gold and silver.

Aztec warriors also took captives. Some captured enemies were used as slaves for a while. But eventually, all captives were sacrificed to the Aztec gods. The Aztecs believed that the gods created people from their own blood. They repaid the gods with human sacrifices.

Every Aztec boy trained to be a warrior. A few became lifelong soldiers, but most also learned other trades such as farming, carpentry, or jewelry making. Girls learned weaving and embroidery. They created beautiful cloaks worn by nobles. Some girls became teachers, healers, or judges in the marketplace. Between ages 12 and 15, Aztec teens attended schools to learn religious songs and dances.

Turn the page.

By 1500 between 200,000 and 300,000 people lived in Tenochtitlan. It was the world's largest city. The great market in Tlatelolco was located just north of Tenochtitlan on the same island. As many as 50,000 people shopped there daily. Market stalls were divided by type, so that all flower sellers were in one place while vendors offering hot tamales and other foods were in another.

The Aztecs traded goods at the market in Tlatelolco, near Tenochtitlan.

The high mountains of central Mexico not only provided lumber and water, but they also were rich with gold. Aztec metalworkers created beautiful golden jewelry, statues, and other objects. When Spanish conquistador Hernán Cortés first arrived in Tenochtitlan, he called it a "city of dreams."

Cortés dreamed of gold. He found it—and more—in Tenochtitlan. What will you find when you visit Tenochtitlan?

⇥To experience life as a merchant's daughter during the middle of the 1400s when the Aztec Empire is growing and expanding, turn to page **13**.

⇥To experience life as the son of a nobleman during the late 1400s when the Aztec Empire is reaching its peak, turn to page **39**.

⇥To experience life as a page under the command of Cortés in the early 1500s, turn to page **71**.

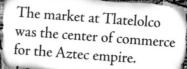

The market at Tlatelolco was the center of commerce for the Aztec empire.

CHAPTER 2

Aztec Girl

"Wait, Zyanya," you call as your cousin races ahead of you toward the market. "We're not children anymore."

Zyanya waits for you to catch up. You make a point of walking slowly, swaying your hips from side to side so that your long skirt swirls around your legs. Your hair, which is nearly shoulder length, swishes as you walk. Now that you are both 12, your mothers have stopped cutting your hair short like a boy's.

Turn the page.

It doesn't take long to reach the great market at Tlatelolco. Auntie Chantico, Zyanya's mother, sells cloaks there. Mother is a marketplace judge. Mother's job is to make sure prices are fair. If disagreements arise, she helps settle them.

You pass rows of market stalls. Everything you could want or need is for sale there—cloth and thread of all colors, pottery, jewelry, meat such as rabbit, deer, or gopher, and even tasty pastries. Thousands of shoppers bargain for goods. There is much trading, and some people use cacao beans or turkey quills filled with gold dust as money. In one row, jewelers sell necklaces of turquoise, silver, and gold.

You stop to look at the earplugs of clay, bone, and seashell. Your ears were pierced during the stretching ceremony when you were 4 years old. The holes were tiny then, but you've stretched them so they are almost big enough for adult earplugs.

At last you reach the street where Auntie Chantico sells her beautiful embroidered cloaks. Her prices are high, but her cloaks are the best.

"Please watch the stall while I do an errand. I am depending on you to make good bargains," she says to you and Zyanya as she rushes away.

Turn the page.

You finger the soft cotton cloaks. Some are pure white. Others are bright red, dipped in dye made from the cochineal bugs that live on the prickly pear cactus. Your father brought these cloaks home from his last trading journey. Auntie sells them for him. Father brings home other treasures too. The best go to the emperor, the great Montezuma.

A woman holds up a white cloak covered with delicate embroidery. "I will give you 300 cacao beans for this cloak," she says. It is a good bargain.

You pull your cousin aside. Something about the way the woman is smiling worries you.

"She doesn't look honest," you say.

"You decide," Zyanya says.

→To sell the cloak to the woman, go to page 17.

→To refuse her offer, turn to page 19.

You go ahead with the sale. When Aunt Chantico returns, you show her the cacao beans. She selects one and pulls it apart. "It's fake," she says. "The chocolate has been removed from the outer husk and replaced with sand."

Cacao beans were used as money to purchase goods and services.

Turn the page.

About half the beans are bad, but the woman has long since disappeared. "You will learn," your aunt says gently.

That evening as you are eating together in the courtyard, your mother says, "Mistakes happen when you are learning. Many people have been fooled. It is my job to remove dishonest traders from the marketplace and report them to the authorities. Would you like to become a marketplace judge like me? Or perhaps you'd rather be a healer. Your Aunt Nenetl will train you to help the sick as she does."

➤To become a healer, turn to page **21**.

➤To train as a marketplace judge, turn to page **22**.

You refuse the woman's offer. When Aunt Chantico returns, she is disappointed. Later, you tell your mother what happened. Mother nods. "The woman's offer was too generous. Some thieves remove the chocolate from the cacao beans and fill the husk with sand. A trader must be alert. It was wise to refuse what seemed like too good an offer."

Mother's basket is overflowing with fresh game meat—frogs, ducks, and a gopher. "Is Father coming home?" you ask.

Mother nods. "Yes, a runner brought the news. We must prepare a fine welcome."

Father is often gone for months at a time on trading trips. When he left, you asked the gods to protect him. His safe return means that your prayers have been answered.

Turn the page.

The homecoming celebrations continue for two days. Father tells of gathering quetzal feathers from traders far to the south. "The emperor will be pleased," Father says, holding up glittery red and green feathers. Father has also brought pottery, jewelry, and more beautiful cloaks for Auntie to sell.

A few days after Father's return, your parents ask if you are ready to begin training with Mother to be a judge in the marketplace. "Or," Father says, "you can continue to work with Auntie Chantico selling the cloaks I've brought home from my trading mission."

➤To become a judge, turn to page **22**.

➤To help Auntie sell cloaks, turn to page **27**.

It is exciting to learn about medicines from Aunt Nenetl. She teaches you how make salve from the prickly pear cactus. It eases pain, helps burns to heal, and prevents wounds from becoming red and swollen. She teaches you about other plants and medicines.

One day you are preparing herbs when a small boy rushes in. "Come help us, please! My brother has fallen into the fire and burned his legs." Your aunt is visiting another neighborhood. If not treated properly, the boy might die.

➠*To search for your aunt, turn to page 25.*

➠*To help the injured boy, turn to page 29.*

You follow Mother through the marketplace. Will you ever be as wise as she is? She teaches you the difference between good cacao beans and poor ones. She makes sure that vendors charge fair prices. When an argument breaks out between two women selling maize, Mother steps in and settles the fight.

Soon after you turn 15, a matchmaker visits your parents. A young man named Necalli wants to marry you. Necalli is 21. He's a merchant like your father, and he's handsome and smart.

At first your parents refuse the matchmaker's offer. They don't want to appear too eager. If they refuse, you will seem an even better catch. The third time the matchmaker asks, your parents agree.

Necalli's parents choose a wedding date that will bring luck. At sunset on the chosen day, your mother and aunts bathe you with soap and sprinkle your face with red and yellow ocher. Then Necalli's family carries you to their home. You sit on a reed mat before the hearth. Necalli joins you.

Necalli's mother brings you a new dress called a huipilli. Your mother gives Necalli a new cape. The matchmaker steps forward and ties a corner of Necalli's cape to your huipilli. Once she has tied the knot, you are married. Now you will begin a new life together.

Turn the page.

muger   varon

Girls typically married between the ages of 15 and 18. Boys were usually several years older.

You move in with Necalli's parents. After the wedding, Necalli and his father leave on a trading mission. "While I am away, you must keep busy," Necalli says. "That way you will not miss me as much. Perhaps you can return to the marketplace and work with your mother. Or you can weave cloaks. I will sell them when I return."

➤ To weave cloaks, turn to page **31**.

➤ To return to work with your mother, turn to page **33**.

24

"I will get my aunt," you say. "She will know what to do."

You race through the streets to find Aunt Nenetl, but by the time you both reach the boy's home, he is dead. Aunt kneels beside the small body and examines his burns. She shakes her head. "Had we treated him quickly, he might have lived. Next time you must not wait for me. Trust yourself. You are a healer."

It is high praise, but her words only add to your guilt. You should have gone directly to help the boy.

Turn the page.

As you are leaving, the family begins preparing the small body for its journey to Mictlan, the Land of the Dead. They wash him, wrap him in a cloth with some favorite items, and burn his body. Later, they'll bury his ashes beneath the floor of the house.

You cannot sleep that night. It's your fault the boy died. The next morning you speak to Aunt Nenetl. "I will help you grow herbs and prepare medicines," you say, "but you must find someone else to care for the sick and injured."

Aunt Nenetl reassures you. "We cannot save everyone. It is up to the gods who lives or dies. Please continue this good work."

➻To continue working with the sick, turn to page **34**.

➻To make medicines, turn to page **35**.

You admire Mother's work as a judge, but you'd rather work as a merchant. After all, you were born under the ninth sign, One Serpent. It is a special sign for merchants. No wonder you were able to spot the fake cacao beans.

A few years after you've begun working, a matchmaker arrives to speak with Father. It is time for you to marry. At first your parents refuse the matchmaker. This makes you seem even more valuable to your future husband. But after some time, they agree that you will marry Tupac. Although he is not yet 23, he has taken two captives in battle. It is an honor to be married to a brave warrior.

When Tupac is not at war, he is a goldsmith like his father. He makes bells and beautiful gold jewelry. After your wedding, you move in with Tupac's family.

Turn the page.

Women wove with imported cotton or with fibers from the maguey plant.

A few weeks later, Tupac leaves for battle. Every evening while he is gone, you weave. The new cloak will be a surprise when he returns home.

One rainy day a few weeks later, Zyanya rushes over to tell you that a runner has returned with news of the battle.

➤To meet the runner, turn to page **36**.

➤To wait until he reaches your neighborhood, turn to page **37**.

"Hurry!" the boy says. You grab some medicine and dash after him.

The injured brother lies in the courtyard beside the fire. He is unconscious. Burns cover much of his lower body.

"I need wet cloths," you say. The family runs to get what you need. You apply the cloths to the burns, cooling the boy's skin. You then cover his legs with salve made from the prickly pear cactus. "You must let him rest," you say. "I will be back to check on him."

When Aunt Nenetl returns, she visits the boy. "You have done well," she tells you. "He might have died from such a serious injury."

Turn the page.

You work with your aunt for several months, learning how to make medicines from plants and herbs. Sometimes you go to market to buy rare plants. Many others grow in Aunt's garden. People begin coming directly to you for help. Aunt doesn't mind. She is getting older and is happy to turn the work over to you.

In a few years' time, you marry and settle into a home of your own. Over the years, your special talent as a healer brings you the respect of your community.

THE END

To follow another path, turn to page 11.
To read the conclusion, turn to page 101.

Like all girls, you learned weaving from your mother at an early age. You find working with cloth peaceful, and you enjoy the long hours sitting at the loom. By the time Necalli returns from his trading mission, you have several cloaks ready for him to sell.

When you become pregnant, the entire family celebrates. They treat you like a queen. Becoming a mother is the most important role in an Aztec woman's life. A midwife helps you during childbirth. She has been present at many births, and it is her job to welcome the baby into the world.

"It is a girl," she cries as the baby is born.

Turn the page.

After a baby's birth, older children would run through the streets, calling out the new baby's name.

When your little girl is 4 days old, the midwife carries the naked child into the courtyard, bathes her, and names her Tlalli. Family and neighbors bring Tlalli gifts—a tiny spindle for weaving and a broom. These gifts reflect the roles she will play as an adult. Someday you will teach Tlalli to use them. But for now, you celebrate her safe arrival with 20 days of feasting.

THE END

To follow another path, turn to page 11.
To read the conclusion, turn to page 101.

Mother is grateful for your help in the marketplace.

Necalli returns in three months and quickly sells his wares. "I must go get more items to sell," he says. "I'll be home again soon."

But this time Necalli doesn't return. Enemy warriors captured him near the coast. You know that a man as young and beautiful as Necalli will be sacrificed to the gods. Your sadness is overwhelming. You can't stop crying.

Perhaps you will marry again. But with so many young men killed or captured in battle, you may not find another husband. You still have your work, though. For now, that will have to be enough.

THE END

To follow another path, turn to page 11.
To read the conclusion, turn to page 101.

33

You agree to try again. You watch as Aunt Nenetl helps people with stomachaches, headaches, and skin rashes. When you mend a small girl's broken arm, Aunt Nenetl says, "You were born to be a healer."

You later marry and have a family of your own. But you continue to care for sick and injured people, following in your aunt's footsteps.

THE END

To follow another path, turn to page 11.
To read the conclusion, turn to page 101.

"I will make medicines," you say. As your skills improve, Aunt Nenetl says, "Now I have more time to treat patients." Your cousin Zyanya opens her own stall at the market selling the lotions and creams that you make.

Soon after you turn 16, you marry a farmer named Matlal. You have bought herbs from him. Now you will move to his farm and begin your own family. "You can still make medicines," Aunt reminds you. But you are busy keeping house, raising children, and helping Matlal with the farm work. You don't forget the skills your aunt taught you, though. You use them to keep your family healthy.

THE END

To follow another path, turn to page 11.
To read the conclusion, turn to page 101.

You're eager to hear the news. Even though the streets are slick with rain, you dash toward the city center, slipping and sliding as you run. There's just one last canal to cross. The boards that form a footbridge over the canal are slippery.

You're fine until you reach the middle of the footbridge. Then you slip and break your arm. You hit the water feet first. "Help me!" you call. You can't swim with an injured arm. But no one comes. As you sink below the surface, your last thoughts are of Tupac. Did he survive the battle? You'll never know. You drown in the cool waters of Lake Texcoco.

THE END

To follow another path, turn to page 11.
To read the conclusion, turn to page 101.

Married women should not run through the streets. The news will reach you soon enough.

When Tupac reaches home, his face is painted red and yellow.

"You have taken another captive?" you ask.

He nods. That makes three total. He's a hero. Now he will attend war councils. Perhaps soon he will become a military officer. You are proud of your husband and eager to become the mother of his children.

THE END

To follow another path, turn to page 11.
To read the conclusion, turn to page 101.

Jaguar knights and
other elite warriors
wore elaborate
costumes to battle.

CHAPTER 3

Noble Youth

Soon after your 10th birthday, Father says, "Next week you will begin attending school for warrior training. Don't be lazy!"

He watches as your head is shaved. One tuft at the back will be your nape lock. You won't cut it until you have captured an enemy warrior.

You work hard studying the history of your people and how to govern. You learn songs and dances that please the gods. You also spend time working in the palace gardens and studying landscaping. Everyone agrees that you have a talent for it. Perhaps when you are too old to fight on the battlefield, you'll design palace gardens. It is a noble profession.

39

Turn the page.

By the time you are 15, you have earned the respect of the other students. Now you will begin weapons training. You will soon be going to war.

First you learn to use projectile weapons, such as bows and arrows, slings, and spear throwers. Usually commoners use these weapons, but even noble warriors must master them.

The telpochcalli was the school that taught military arts and other trades.

You also practice using an arrow launcher called an atlatl. It looks like a stick with a notch at one end. A dart is placed into a groove carved along the atlatl's length. The notch holds it in place. When the warrior makes a throwing motion, the dart sails toward the enemy. It takes practice to throw the dart accurately.

Today you'll practice with shock weapons, which are used in close combat. One group of students will be trained on the two-handed sword called the macuahuitl. It has sharp cutting edges made of obsidian, a volcanic glass. The other group will learn to use the tepoztopilli, a thrusting spear.

➤To use the macuahuitl, turn to page **42**.

➤To use the tepoztopilli, turn to page **44**.

A successful warrior named Zolton teaches you how to use the macuahuitl.

"Careful," Zolton says. "The obsidian blades running along both sides are sharp."

"It is a deadly weapon," he continues. "But your job is not to kill the enemy. You must capture him alive." Killing an enemy may save your life, but capturing him alive will bring you honor.

By the time you are 18, you have mastered this weapon and many others. It is time to observe battle firsthand.

As you prepare to go to war, your friend Luc asks if you are afraid.

"No," you say quickly. "To die in battle is an honor." You have been taught that death on the battlefield brings great reward. For four years after you die, you will follow the sun across the sky from morning to noon. Then you will return to earth as a butterfly or hummingbird.

"A great honor," Luc agrees, "but perhaps we should continue to practice."

➤ *To practice, turn to page 45.*

➤ *To rest before battle, turn to page 46.*

You join the group training on the tepoztopilli. "You don't throw it," the instructor says. "You thrust it at the enemy, crippling him so that he surrenders. Taking captives will bring you honor."

You continue to practice with various weapons—the bow and arrow, knife, atlatl, and of course, the tepoztopilli. Hard physical labor prepares your body for battle. At last, when you turn 18, you are allowed to observe a battle.

Your father will pay a seasoned warrior to take you under his care. He asks if you prefer an Eagle Knight or a Jaguar Knight. Jaguar and Eagle Knights are members of elite military orders. They've proven themselves in battle.

➧ *To go with an Eagle Knight, turn to page **48**.*

➧ *To go with a Jaguar Knight, turn to page **52**.*

"Let's practice," you say, heading for a hidden corner of the courtyard.

You hold a shield before your face as protection. Luc slashes the air with his macuahuitl. He will not harm you, at least not on purpose. But he is tired. At the last minute, he lets go. The macuahuitl flies at you!

You leap backward, tripping over a rock and twisting your leg. You cry out in pain.

"I'll get help," Luc calls.

"No, wait!" You worry that if your teachers discover that you are injured, you won't be allowed to go to battle. Maybe you should see if the leg heals itself in the next few days.

→To wait for the leg to heal, turn to page **65**.

→To summon a healer, turn to page **66**.

You decide against more practice. Your father arranges for you to go to battle with Coatl, a man of great courage. You will carry his weapons and supplies to the battlefield.

On the day you march to battle, you meet at sunrise. "You'll watch the battle from the hillside," Coatl says. From your high-up place, you see the two armies approach one another. When they are about 15 feet apart, the archers release their arrows.

Warriors tried to take as many captives as possible during hand-to-hand combat.

When they run out of arrows, warriors with atlatls send darts at the enemy. It only takes a few minutes to fire the projectiles. Then the archers run to safety. Now the elite warriors begin hand-to-hand combat. You hear the thud of spears against wooden shields. Battle cries fill the air.

The fighting doesn't last long. There are many captives.

You return to Tenochtitlan with the triumphant warriors and the doomed captives. Emperor Ahuitzotl is pleased. All of Tenochtitlan celebrates. A few days later, the captives are sacrificed to the god of the sun and war.

Your father is proud. He asks you if you are ready to marry.

➻*To marry, turn to page 56.*

➻*To wait, turn to page 57.*

"I'd like to be an Eagle Knight someday," you say. Your father chooses an Eagle Knight named Coatl to guide you during the first battle. You carry his supplies and prepare his food during the long march to battle.

War does not happen by surprise. Ambassadors from Tenochtitlan have pleaded with a neighboring city to pay tribute to your emperor, Ahuitzotl. But they would rather fight than give in to the mighty Tenochtitlan ruler.

And so the battle begins. First archers and dart throwers hurl projectiles at the enemy. The enemy warriors shoot arrows and darts back at your warriors. The weapons thud against the wooden shields. Then the best warriors enter the battle. You watch from the hillside, eager for the day when you can join the fight.

The battle won, you return in triumph to Tenochtitlan. You go to the temple to watch the sacrifice of captives. Some must be pushed up the pyramid stairs. Others walk bravely to their deaths. The crowd cheers as the priest rips the heart from a captive's chest and lifts it up to the sun god.

You meet friends at the temple. "Come with us," they say. "We will celebrate." One of the boys, Tenoch, has pulque, a kind of beer that farmers and city workers drink.

"It is against the rules," you say. "If someone finds out …"

"No one will ever know," Tenoch says.

➼*To join them, turn to page 50.*
➼*To return to school, turn to page 54.*

You wander through the streets with Tenoch, but when he offers you a drink, you refuse. "Public drunkenness is punishable by death," you warn, but Tenoch only scoffs.

No matter what you say, Tenoch answers with teasing words. You're tired of his teasing. "I'll see you tomorrow," you say, as you return to the school.

It is two days before you see one of the boys who had been drinking the pulque. He walks with a limp, and his ears are bleeding.

"What happened?" you ask.

"One of the instructors caught us with pulque. I was beaten and pierced with maguey spines," he says. "Tenoch nearly died of his beating. He has been thrown out of the school permanently."

You're very glad you returned to the school when you did.

Your teachers announce that another war is near. Coatl encourages you. "This is your chance to take a captive. Be confident."

It takes a few days to reach the battlefield. Despite Coatl's encouraging words, you don't feel confident. The battle is about to begin. You must decide whether to step forward or not.

→To fight, turn to page **60**.

→To watch, turn to page **68**.

Your older brother, Xipilli, is a Jaguar Knight. He will be your guide in battle. He insists that you observe the first battle from a distance. By the second battle, you are ready to join the attack.

"Choose someone your age," Xipilli says. "You'll have a better chance that way. Remember, the goal is not to kill—it is to capture the enemy. That will please the emperor and the gods."

Jaguar Knights wore jaguar skins. Eagle Knights wore feathers.

Noise surrounds you. Weapons clunk against wooden shields. Warriors shout out the names of their towns. From time to time, a warrior screams as he falls wounded. You find a warrior who looks about your age. He's alone in an area away from the main battle. You sneak forward, your shield in one hand and your spear in the other.

As you close in, your heart races and your hand sweats as it grips the polished wood of your weapon. You lunge at your enemy. At the same moment, he lunges toward you. Your spear bounces off his shield, but his hits its mark. Your shoulder burns where the blade struck.

53

➤ *To drop your weapon, turn to page* **62**.

➤ *To strike again, turn to page* **64**.

You return to school and prepare for the next battle. You practice many hours with your weapons. You study warfare and talk to experienced warriors. You even cut your ears with maguey thorns until they bleed. Such sacrifices please the gods.

This time you will fight. As a new warrior, you cannot wear body armor or paint your face. All you have is a shield to protect you. You carry a knife and the tepoztopilli. Your teachers said that you may work with five or six other new warriors for your first capture.

The commander sounds the conch shell. The battle is on. Arrows and darts fly through the air. As the archers retreat, skilled warriors take the field. At last it is time for you to advance. Your friends are waiting for you to join them for a group capture.

The hornlike sound of a conch shell signaled the start of a battle.

➤To join them, turn to page **59**.

➤To act alone, turn to page **60**.

"Yes, I want to marry." Your parents consult your teachers and relatives to find a suitable bride. Then they hire a matchmaker to approach the girl's parents. You won't meet the girl until your wedding day.

Your bride, Atzi, is of noble birth, and she's lovely. Atzi moves into your father's palace to begin married life.

Your mother is pleased by the prospect of grandchildren. You're eager to have a family, but you also look forward to returning to the battlefield. You will bring honor to your family and your emperor.

THE END

To follow another path, turn to page 11.
To read the conclusion, turn to page 101.

You are still young. You ask your father's permission to wait before marrying. First you want to make your mark as a great warrior.

In a first battle, young warriors may team up to take a captive. When the day of your first battle arrives, you join five other new warriors and successfully capture an enemy. When you return to the city, the emperor calls you to the palace. Now that you have proved yourself, you cut your nape lock.

During the next battle, you take a captive on your own. When you are taken to see the emperor, your face is painted red. The emperor's tribute collectors add yellow paint to your temples. From now on you may wear warrior's clothing even during peacetime.

Turn the page.

As your family celebrates the victory, you tell them that you are ready to marry. Because you come from a royal family, your father arranges a royal marriage. You will marry the daughter of the king whose city you helped to conquer. Someday your son will become the leader there. He will bring honor to the empire as you have done.

58

THE END

To follow another path, turn to page 11.
To read the conclusion, turn to page 101.

There is strength in numbers. Your group moves on to the battlefield. "There," one of them shouts. He points to a lone enemy warrior, not much older than you are.

When you are within reach, you lash out, striking his knee. He strikes back, but the others help you overpower him. He cries out and gives up.

Men with ropes rush forward, taking your captive to the rear.

You return to the city rejoicing. Because you have taken a captive, you cut your nape lock and paint your face. Now you are a man. You'll soon earn the rank of Eagle Knight.

THE END

To follow another path, turn to page 11.
To read the conclusion, turn to page 101.

You step onto the battlefield alone and choose your opponent. You prepare to thrust the tepoztopilli at him, but he manages to strike first. You collapse and fall to the ground. Your enemy stands over you, ready to strike again. You have no choice but to surrender.

An Aztec priest prepares for a sacrifice.

You know what awaits—your death as a sacrifice to the gods. Capturing an enemy brings honor. Death on the battlefield brings honor. But death as a captive brings only sorrow and pain.

Two days later, you are marched to the pyramid. The man ahead of you faints, but you remain strong as you climb to the top of the pyramid. Several priests are waiting. They grab you and lower you to a stone table. The last thing you see is the obsidian knife high in the air above your heart.

61

THE END

To follow another path, turn to page 11.
To read the conclusion, turn to page 101.

You drop your weapon and sink to the ground, expecting to become a captive. But Xipilli slips in beside you. He strikes out, knocking down the enemy and taking him captive.

You lie on the ground, clutching your wounded shoulder. Men rush onto the field to tie up the enemy captive, and Xipilli moves on. A priest washes your wound and applies a salve made of healing herbs and plants. Then he bandages it with a clean cloth. You will survive, although your arm is severely damaged. Despite your pain, you're glad that your army won the battle.

After the battle, your fellow warriors carry you home on a litter. Your arm will take weeks to heal, and it will never be as strong as before. Your days as a warrior are over, but you will lead a rewarding life as the emperor's favorite landscape gardener. Your gardens become famous and bring pleasure to all who see them.

THE END

To follow another path, turn to page 11.
To read the conclusion, turn to page 101.

Despite the pain, you strike out again. But your arm is weak. You are bleeding heavily and you fall to the ground. The battle continues around you. You no longer hear the war cries as the life drains out of you. You focus instead on the swirl of bright colors from tribal banners, decorated cloaks, and the painted faces of warriors. Then you close your eyes for the last time. Your death on the battlefield will bring you honor.

64

THE END

To follow another path, turn to page 11.
To read the conclusion, turn to page 101.

"Let's wait," you say. "Help me to my room."

Luc does his best to help you. He brings food and drink and makes excuses so that no one misses you.

But by the next day, you have developed a fever. Your leg is swollen and hot, and you moan with pain. Finally your friend calls a priest.

The priest prays over you and offers various medicines, but the leg gets worse. Despite their best efforts, the healers cannot help you. You die on a mat in your room at school, never having experienced the excitement of battle.

65

THE END

To follow another path, turn to page 11.
To read the conclusion, turn to page 101.

"Go ahead and get help," you moan.

Luc finds a priest who is also a healer. The priest applies a healing salve, splints the leg, and carries you to your room. Unfortunately, the leg does not heal well. You walk with a limp, and you can no longer run.

"You'll never be a warrior," Father says, disappointment clouding his face. "This accident must be a sign from the gods. You will prove yourself in other ways."

You return to the palace gardens and study with the royal landscape gardener. Someday you will be in charge of designing the emperor's gardens.

Crops and gardens were difficult to grow on the swampy island and were therefore highly valued.

THE END

To follow another path, turn to page 11.
To read the conclusion, turn to page 101.

You hesitate at first. When the battle begins, the highest-ranking warriors enter the battlefield first. Eagle and Jaguar knights follow them. Finally it is your turn, and you feel ready to enter the battle.

Successful, costumed warriors entered the battle before lower ranking warriors.

The battlefield is strewn with bodies. You crouch low and approach a warrior who looks to be about your age. You jab at him with your spear. He jabs back, but his aim is better than yours. He plunges the spear into your thigh.

You look down to see blood spurting from your leg. You grab the wound, but cannot stop the bleeding. You collapse on the battlefield, the life quickly draining from your body. It is a noble death. Your last thoughts are hopeful ones. You imagine yourself as a hummingbird living forever, favored by the gods.

THE END

To follow another path, turn to page 11.
To read the conclusion, turn to page 101.

Montezuma II greeted Hernán Cortés in Tenochtitlan.

Spanish Page

You are 12 years old. Your family moved from Spain to the Spanish colony of Cuba a year ago so your father could work for the governor. One day your father announces that he has found a position for you as a page. "Hernán Cortés is leading an expedition to New Spain. You will go with him."

On February 19, 1519, you leave Cuba with Cortés. He brings 11 ships, 508 soldiers, 17 horses, and several large mastiff dogs. There are weapons, too—cannons and guns. Will there be trouble ahead?

71

Turn the page.

You do whatever Cortés asks—fetch supplies, polish his boots, and check on the horses. You stay on the ship when Cortés goes ashore at Cozumel, where many Tabascan people live. He returns with gifts from the Tabascans, including several female slaves.

Cortés orders the ships to head northwest. "We're going to find gold," he says.

Even before you reach shore, royal visitors arrive bearing more gifts. They speak an unfamiliar language. But one of the Tabascan slaves understands them. "They are Aztec nobles," she says. "The great emperor Montezuma II sent them."

Cortés' eyes sparkle with pleasure as he admires the jewelry, cloaks, and feather work they've brought. He looks at the young slave girl and asks her name. "Malinche," she replies shyly.

From that moment on, Malinche remains at Cortés' side to translate the words of the Aztec leaders. It's not easy. She translates the Nahuatl language of the Aztecs into the Mayan language. Then a Mayan-speaking priest named Aguilar translates it into Spanish. But Malinche is smart and quickly learns Spanish. Soon Aguilar no longer needs to translate.

When Montezuma's ambassadors return, they bring more gifts of gold. "Take these gifts and go," they say. But Cortés has no intention of leaving. He plans to find Montezuma's city of gold.

It takes three months of travel through mountain passes to reach the capital city of Tenochtitlan. At last you see it in the valley below. You enter the city on one of three causeways—raised paths across the lake.

Turn the page.

The great Montezuma climbs out of a golden litter carried by servants. He's wearing a cloak embroidered with golden threads and an enormous feathered headdress. After the leaders exchange greetings, Montezuma takes Cortés to the Palace Axayacatl, the former home of Montezuma's father. It's the most elegant building you've ever seen. It's large enough for Cortés and all his men to stay there.

The next afternoon Montezuma invites Cortés to visit his palace. Malinche will serve as translator. You can go if you want.

→To go to Montezuma's palace, go to page **75**.
→To wait at the Palace Axayacatl, turn to page **78**.

You follow Cortés and Malinche to Montezuma's palace. The palace's long hallways lead to hundreds of rooms grouped around three huge courtyards. He shows you the fabulous grounds and the rare animals in the zoo.

On the return to Palace Axayacatl, you overhear Cortés speaking with his officers. "The men are getting restless," a captain says.

"This place is dangerous," says another. "We are trapped on an island. Montezuma could order us all killed."

"Don't worry. I will soon take him prisoner," says Cortés.

The next afternoon Cortés, Malinche, the captains, and 30 well-armed soldiers return to Montezuma's palace. You go along.

Turn the page.

You have begun to learn a few words of Nahuatl, the Aztec language. Knowing the language is useful, especially when you meet Montezuma or his warriors.

You're surprised when Cortés accuses Montezuma of attacking the Spanish settlement of Veracruz on the coast. "I have no desire to start a war or to destroy Tenochtitlan. Everything will be forgiven, if you come with us. You will be as well served and attended as in your own palace," Cortés tells him.

At first, Montezuma protests. After several hours of argument, he agrees to go, but not as a prisoner. He informs his people that he is going to stay with Cortés to learn more about the Spanish and their ways. Only then does the mighty emperor call for his royal litter and ride to the Palace Axayacatl with Cortés.

For the next five months, Montezuma rules his people from Axayacatl. But there is no doubt he is a prisoner. Anyone wishing to speak to Montezuma must get permission from Cortés.

One day Malinche overhears Montezuma planning a revolt with his military advisers. She tells Cortés. When Cortés confronts Montezuma, the Aztec leader confesses. He adds that his runners saw 18 Spanish warships anchored off the coast at Veracruz. The ships belong to Diego de Velázquez, the governor of Cuba. Pánfilo de Narváez is in command. He and Velázquez plan to challenge Cortés over Aztec gold.

Cortés splits his forces. Some will remain in Tenochtitlan guarding Montezuma. The rest will go with Cortés to confront Narváez.

➤*To go with Cortés, turn to page* **82**.

➤*To stay in Tenochtitlan, turn to page* **83**.

You have work to do organizing supplies, so you stay at the palace. When Cortés returns, he brings word that Montezuma has given permission for the Spanish to roam the city freely. You've learned some Nahuatl by listening to Malinche and the servants. Perhaps it is time to explore the city on your own.

You go to the marketplace. Thousands of shoppers barter for goods. Canoes shuttle back and forth from one shore to the other, bringing fruits and vegetables to market. One farmer carries dozens of purple flowers from his flat-bottomed canoe to a flower vendor's stall.

Beyond the marketplace, you notice that the homes become smaller. Women sit in the courtyards visiting and caring for children. Canals allow canoes to travel throughout the city. Boards laid from one side to the other form bridges so you can walk over the canals.

When you reach the lakeshore, you see several of the flat-bottomed canoes pulled up at the water's edge. You are tempted to borrow one and try rowing around the lake. Is anyone watching?

➤*To return to the palace, turn to page **80**.*

➤*To take a canoe, turn to page **92**.*

"Where have you been?" one of the officers asks back at the palace. "While you were out, Cortés has taken Montezuma prisoner."

"Prisoner?"

"Yes. We feared an uprising of the Aztecs. We feel trapped on this island. Cortés convinced Montezuma to come here so we can keep an eye on him."

Cortés took Montezuma prisoner in 1520.

Weeks pass. You spend time with Montezuma. He seems to enjoy your company. You are one of the few Spanish who can speak Nahuatl.

One day Cortés rushes into Montezuma's chambers. "Out, boy!" he says.

You later learn that Montezuma and his nobles had been planning a revolt. Montezuma also told Cortés that Diego de Velázquez, the governor of Cuba, was planning to challenge Cortés. At first Velázquez had supported Cortés, but now he wanted the gold for himself.

Cortés tells his troops, "Get ready to march!" When you begin packing supplies, he takes you aside and orders you to remain in Tenochtitlan. Malinche is going with him. Someone who speaks Nahuatl must stay behind.

Turn to page **83**.

You go with Cortés and 350 soldiers to confront Narváez. Just outside the city of Tlaxcala, you meet Andrés de Duero, a friend of Cortés who had helped him plan the expedition. Duero is Governor Velázquez's secretary.

Cortés offers Duero and his soldiers gifts of gold if they will desert Velázquez. The men accept his offer and tell Cortés the exact location of Narváez and his men.

Even though it's pouring rain and the ground is slick with mud, Cortés leads his men on. "We attack tonight," he says. He orders Malinche to wait in a ravine along with the food and equipment.

➻To go with Malinche, turn to page **89**.

➻To remain with Cortés, turn to page **98**.

You stay at the palace. Captain Alvarado is in charge. Cortés has left 120 men to guard the city and the emperor.

The big Festival of Toxcatl is about to begin. Montezuma asks Alvarado to allow the people to celebrate. The festival occurs every May to honor the Aztec god Tezcatlipoca. It's a time of praying for rain to fill the rivers and nourish the crops. It's also a time of human sacrifices. But Montezuma knows that Cortés does not approve of human sacrifice. If Alvarado forbids the celebration, Montezuma fears the people will rebel.

"There will be no sacrifices," Montezuma promises Alvarado.

Turn the page.

As you walk around the city with Alvarado, you see captives held in cages near the temple. One of the Aztec statues holds a paper banner drenched in blood. Despite Montezuma's promises, it looks as if the priests are planning human sacrifices. Alvarado is worried but agrees to allow the celebration.

On the fourth day of the celebration, Alvarado and his soldiers gather weapons and put on their armor. "What's happening?" you ask.

"Tonight is the Serpent Dance at the Patio of Dances," one soldier says. "The captain has heard rumors that the Aztecs are planning a revolt."

"Sixty men will guard the palace," another soldier says. "Sixty will go with Alvarado." You are not a fighter, but you could go along and help fire the cannons.

➤To go to the Patio of Dances, go to page **85**.

➤To stay and guard the palace, turn to page **86**.

You follow the soldiers to the Patio of Dances. Drums beat, flutes play, and about 500 dancers sway. You stand near one of the gates as hundreds of Aztec nobles and warriors file into the patio. Spanish soldiers surround the patio.

Suddenly the Spanish soldiers close the gates, trapping everyone inside. The soldiers run into the crowd with their swords, killing everyone they meet. The crowd panics. They are unarmed. It's a massacre! The brilliant green quetzal feathers on the dancers' costumes turn red with blood. You are too sickened to move.

A soldier pushes you aside. "Go!" he yells.

Turn to page 95.

You stay at the palace. Suddenly, screams pierce the night. It's coming from the Patio of Dances. "What's happening?" The screaming turns to wailing, and the entire city seems to be at the palace gates.

"We're under siege," an officer says. "The Aztecs are attacking."

"Attacking?" you ask, but the soldiers are too busy fighting to answer. Later, you learn that Alvarado and his men attacked first at the Patio of Dances. Thousands of Aztecs died.

For days, Aztec warriors storm the palace gates. You run out of food, and the water is nearly gone. Alvarado sends a messenger under cover of darkness to find Cortés and bring him back. Cortés arrives just in time and manages to create a temporary truce.

But Montezuma is a defeated man. Alvarado has placed him in leg irons. He is no longer an impressive king—only a captive. His gold belongs to the Spanish, and soon his city will too. You try to comfort the emperor, but it's useless. Even you can see that the day will soon come when the Aztecs and Spanish fight to the death.

On July 1, 1520, Cortés insists that Montezuma go to the rooftop of the palace to talk to his people. But who can hear him over the Aztec drumming and stone throwing? Even Montezuma is not safe. A rock hits him on the head. Had the stone thrower meant to hit a Spanish soldier? Probably. But it is Montezuma who falls.

Turn the page.

"Montezuma!" you cry as the soldiers carry him to safety. He survives for three days but refuses the food and drink you offer. When Montezuma dies, you feel as if you have lost a favorite uncle.

Within a year, the empire collapses. Cortés is in charge now. As the work of rebuilding begins, Cortés sends another treasure shipment to Spain.

88

Montezuma was fatally injured on the rooftop of the Palace Axayacatl.

➥ *To sail to Spain with the gold, turn to page **93**.*

➥ *To remain in Mexico, turn to page **94**.*

It's a relief when one of the officers comes to get you and Malinche. "The battle is over," he says. "Narváez surrendered."

You barely reach Cortés when a messenger arrives. "You are needed at Tenochtitlan," he says. "Captain Alvarado feared a revolt, so he attacked the Aztecs during the ceremony. Thousands died. Alvarado and his men are trapped in the palace without food or water."

Cortés races to Tenochtitlan. It's like a ghost town. The people have gone into hiding. Alvarado's men are starving after days without food. They cheer when Cortés arrives.

Cortés cannot persuade Montezuma to open the markets to get his soldiers food. However, Montezuma tricks Cortés into believing that Montezuma's brother Cuitláhuac, who is also a prisoner, can help.

Turn the page.

As soon as Cortés releases him, Cuitláhuac calls in warriors from distant cities and villages. The next morning, they begin attacking the Palace Axayacatl, where you are staying.

The Aztec war cries frighten you. Even worse, the Aztecs throw stones over the palace walls. It's as if stones are raining from the sky. The Aztecs send flaming arrows into the courtyard too.

Cortés orders the cannons fired. His crossbowmen send volleys of arrows at the enemy, but still the fighting continues. A warrior rushes through the gate toward Cortés and attacks him. Cortés slumps against the wall.

➤ To call for help, go to page **91**.

➤ To rush to Cortés' aid, turn to page **97**.

You report what you've seen to one of Cortés' captains. He sends two soldiers to help Cortés to safety. The conquistador is bleeding. But his wounds are not serious. As soon as you bandage him, he rushes back to the battle.

The fighting continues throughout the next day, but you barely know what's happening. At last an officer tells you, "We leave at midnight for Tlaxcala. We'll take as much gold as we can. Fill your pockets."

But Cortés warns, "Better not to overload yourselves. He who travels safest in the dark night travels lightest."

→To carry two bags of gold, turn to page **96**.
→To take only one gold necklace, turn to page **99**.

You push the canoe into the water and begin to row. The lake is huge. You find that rowing is hard work. You're getting very tired. The sun is beginning to set. You are almost to the other side when you hear a noise. Is that an enemy lying in wait? Fear makes you move quickly. You turn the boat around and begin rowing in the other direction. But your arms are weak and shaky, and you're confused in the dark.

Another noise frightens you, and when you jump, the boat rocks. You lose your balance and tumble into the lake. "Help!" you cry as you sink beneath the water. You cannot swim. Your last thoughts are of your family as you drown in Lake Texcoco.

THE END

To follow another path, turn to page 11.
To read the conclusion, turn to page 101.

You volunteer to go along. It will be good to see your relatives still living in Spain.

"Guard my gold," Cortés says as you leave. You fully intend to do so. But just before you reach Spain, French pirates attack the ship.

You reach for a sword to protect the gold. But before you pick it up, one of the pirates pushes the point of his weapon into your chest. He tosses you overboard. You sink to the bottom of the sea, another victim of the quest for Aztec gold.

93

THE END

To follow another path, turn to page 11.
To read the conclusion, turn to page 101.

You like Mexico. It's your home now.

Spain's King Charles names Cortés governor and captain-general of New Spain. Cortés is responsible for rebuilding the city and exploring other lands in America. He sends troops to Guatemala and Honduras. You remain at his side and become an important member of his household. You advise him on matters related to his household and day-to-day life in Tenochtitlan, now renamed Mexico City.

In a few years, you marry an Aztec woman and raise several children. They grow up speaking both Spanish and the Aztec language of Nahuatl.

94

THE END

To follow another path, turn to page 11.
To read the conclusion, turn to page 101.

You run and hide in a dark alley. Wails echo through the city. A loud voice begins to call, "Mexicanos, come running! The strangers have murdered our people!"

Warriors rush from their homes armed with shields and spears. You huddle against a hut, trying to disappear. But a boy finds you there. His yell brings others who hit you with sticks, tie you up, and drag you to the temple. You're killed quickly by a priest's knife, and your heart is offered to the gods.

THE END

To follow another path, turn to page 11.
To read the conclusion, turn to page 101.

You grab several bags of gold. At least you'll have no money problems in the future. But the gold is heavy, and you fall far behind the others. Suddenly out of the darkness appears a painted warrior. He swings his weapon at you, catching you in the knee. You fall to the ground. As you struggle to get up, the warrior drives his spear into your chest. You die instantly.

The Aztecs made gold, stone, and turquoise statues of the fire god Xiuhtecuhtli.

THE END

To follow another path, turn to page 11.
To read the conclusion, turn to page 101.

You rush to Cortés. So does Captain Alvarado. "Help me get him inside," Alvarado says.

As you reach out to help Cortés, a rock smashes into your head. You slump to the ground. Feeling your head, you discover it is bleeding. You're dizzy and your legs don't work. The last thing you see before you die is Captain Alvarado helping Cortés to safety.

THE END

To follow another path, turn to page 11.
To read the conclusion, turn to page 101.

When fighting begins, you realize that you should have gone with Malinche. If you had, you'd be safe. Cortés is on horseback leading his troops. You are on foot and without a weapon. Your only hope is to run into the forest and hide. But as you run, something heavy hits your head. It knocks you to the ground.

You feel sick when you stand up, but you keep walking. Getting to safety drives you forward. One of Cortés' soldiers finds you staggering alone.

"What happened?" he asks.

"My head," you moan.

"Lie down," he says. "You'll be fine after you rest." But you're not. The pain in your head increases. By morning you are dead from a fractured skull.

THE END

To follow another path, turn to page 11.
To read the conclusion, turn to page 101.

It is dark when you slip the necklace around your neck and follow the guards past the Pyramid of the Sun. When you reach the giant causeway at Tacuba, soldiers must repair damaged sections of the bridge so that you can cross. You're nearly across when an Aztec woman suddenly yells, "Mexicanos! Come running! Our enemies are escaping!"

You escape the island just before canoes full of Aztec warriors enter the water. You huddle in safety with Malinche and the priests. Cortés leads his troops into battle. Nearly 600 of his men die that night. So do hundreds of Aztecs.

After the battle, you begin the march to the friendly city of Tlaxcala, 50 miles away. Cortés is already making plans to retake Tenochtitlan.

THE END

To follow another path, turn to page 11.
To read the conclusion, turn to page 101.

Today a plaza in Mexico City stands near the ruins of Tenochtitlan.

CHAPTER 5

The End of An Empire

Hernán Cortés, the Spanish conquistador, not only ended the reign of the Aztec rulers, but he also destroyed their great city. Thousands of Tenochtitlan's people died in the final battles.

Montezuma died too. The Spanish believed that he died of a head wound caused by rocks the Aztecs threw at Spanish soldiers. The Aztecs, however, claimed that the Spanish killed him. The survivors saw Spanish soldiers destroy their homes, topple their pyramids, and steal their remaining treasures.

As terrible as the fighting was, a worse enemy was looming. The Spanish had brought the deadly smallpox with them. The Aztecs had no resistance to the disease, and they died by the thousands. In some areas, half of the people died of smallpox. Many others starved to death, too sick to find food. Cuitláhuac, who became emperor after Montezuma II, died of smallpox on December 4, 1520.

Cuauhtémoc, nephew of Cuitláhuac and Montezuma, became the last emperor of the Aztecs. Cortés and his soldiers conquered the city a final time in 1521. The people fled. The city was destroyed.

Much of the Aztec gold was lost. In the last days of the Empire, Aztec warriors dumped baskets of gold into Lake Texcoco. The gold Cortés found was melted down and sent to Spain. But much of it never arrived. Some loads were lost at sea, and French pirates took the rest.

The Spanish were horrified by the Aztec practice of human sacrifice. Cortés and his men watched captives taken to the top of a pyramid and forced onto a stone table. The Aztecs believed that blood sacrifices convinced the gods to provide for them. While four priests held the captive down, another pierced his chest with a sharp knife and removed the heart. The priest then held the heart in the air as an offering to the gods.

To Cortés' horror, some of his own men became victims of sacrifice after battles with Aztec warriors. Stopping this practice became one of his goals. Cortés set up Roman Catholic shrines. Spanish priests baptized natives in every conquered town or city. After the conquest Catholic priests established churches and schools to convert the natives. Today most Mexicans practice the Roman Catholic faith.

Some Catholic priests realized that valuable Aztec knowledge had been lost. They gathered artists and storytellers to create books of drawings about their life in the time before Cortés arrived. Much of what we now know about the Aztecs comes from these books.

More than 1 million people in Mexico still speak the Nahuatl language. Tourists who visit Mexico can tour the ruins of Aztec pyramids and temples or take a boat ride on canals dug by Aztec farmers.

Mexico gave us tortillas, tamales, and tomatoes, as well as hot cocoa. Modern doctors use several Aztec medicines to treat diseases. Aztec artists created beautiful works of art and woven cloth. The red dye that the Aztecs made from the cochineal bugs is still used. Even though the Aztec Empire ended 400 years ago, it continues to influence our daily lives.

TIMELINE

AD 1100—The Aztecs leave their home in Aztlan.

1100–1200s—The Aztecs reach central Mexico and establish city-states in the valleys and plains surrounding the Valley of Mexico.

1325—The city of Tenochtitlan is founded on an island in Lake Texcoco in the Valley of Mexico.

1325–1428—The Aztecs construct a dike and canal system in Tenochtitlan; Texcoco and Tlacopan join with Tenochtitlan to form the Triple Alliance; Acamapichtli becomes the first king of the Aztec Empire.

1390—Construction of Templo Mayor, the major pyramid, begins in Tenochtitlan.

1440—Montezuma I begins a 28-year reign.

1450–1452—A severe drought destroys the harvest, causing thousands of people to starve.

1473—The Aztecs conquer Tlatelolco, a neighboring city.

1502—Montezuma II, the most well-known Aztec king, is crowned.

1519—Hernán Cortés arrives on the coast of Mexico in March; he establishes Veracruz; he reaches Tenochtitlan in November and enters the city as a guest of Montezuma.

1520—Cortés begins an assault on the Aztec Empire; Montezuma dies; the next emperor, Cuitláhuac, drives the Spanish out of the city before dying of smallpox.

1521—Spanish and Tlaxcalans attack Tenochtitlan and conquer the city; the last emperor, Cuauhtémoc, surrenders to Cortés on August 13.

1522—The Spanish rebuild Tenochtitlan as Mexico City, capital of New Spain; Cortés becomes the governor of New Spain.

OTHER PATHS TO EXPLORE

In this book you've seen how the events of the past look different from three points of view. Perspectives on history are as varied as the people who lived it. Seeing history from many points of view is an important part of understanding it.

Here are some ideas for other points of view to explore:

+ The Aztec city-states were always at war with neighboring city-states. The winner demanded victims for sacrifice from these towns. How would life change if you lived in constant fear of being sacrificed?

+ Soldiers, sailors, and servants chose to go to the Americas with the conquistadors. If you were living then, would you have been likely to go?

+ Imagine you lived in Tenochtitlan at the time of the conquest. People from a distant country move in and destroy your home. They refuse to allow you to practice your religion. Would you be quick to change or would you cling to your old ways as long as possible?

READ MORE

Cooke, Tim. *National Geographic Investigates Ancient Aztec: Archaeology Unlocks the Secrets of Mexico's Past.* Washington, D.C.: National Geographic, 2007.

Green, Jen. *Hail! Aztecs.* New York: Crabtree Pub., 2011.

Guillain, Charlotte. *Aztec Warriors.* Chicago: Raintree, 2010.

Heinrichs, Ann. *The Aztecs.* New York: Marshall Cavendish Benchmark, 2012.

Raum, Elizabeth. *What Did the Aztecs do for Me?* Chicago: Heinemann, 2011.

INTERNET SITES

Use FactHound to find Internet sites related to this book. All of the sites on FactHound have been researched by our staff.

Here's all you do:
Visit *www.facthound.com*
Type in this code: 9781429647793

Glossary

ambassador (am-BA-suh-duhr)—a government official who represents his or her country

conquistador (kon-KEYS-tuh-dor)—a military leader in the Spanish conquest of North and South America during the 1500s

convert (kuhn-VURT)—to change from one religion or faith to another

elite (i-LEET)—a group of people who have special advantages or talents

embroidery (im-BROY-duh-ree)—a form of sewing used to sew pictures or designs on cloth

litter (LIT-ur)—a stretcher for carrying a wounded person

maguey (mu-GAY)—a type of agave plant with spines

ocher (OH-ker)—yellow or reddish-yellow iron ore or other earth materials used to color something

quetzal (ket-SAHL)—a red and green bird that is the national bird of Guatemala

salve (SAV)—medicine or lotion that relieves pain and helps heal wounds or burns

truce (TROOS)—an agreement to stop fighting in a war

turquoise (TUR-koiz)—a blue-green gemstone

BIBLIOGRAPHY

Boone, Elizabeth Hill. *The Aztec World*. Washington, D.C.: Smithsonian Books, 1994.

Carrasco, Davíd. *Daily Life of The Aztecs: People of the Sun and Earth*. Westport, Conn.: Greenwood Press, 1998.

Clendinnen, Inga. *Aztecs*. New York: Cambridge U.P., 1991.

Levy, Buddy. *Conquistador: Hernán Cortés, King Montezuma, and the Last Stand of the Aztecs*. New York: Bantam, 2008.

Marks, Richard Lee. *Cortés: The Great Adventurer and the Fate of Aztec Mexico*. New York: Alfred A. Knopf, 1993.

Marrin, Albert. *Aztecs and Spaniards: Cortés and the Conquest of Mexico*. New York: Atheneum, 1986.

Smith, Michael E. *The Aztecs*. Oxford: Blackwell, 1996.

Teresi, Dick. *Lost Discoveries: The Ancient Roots of Modern Science—from the Babylonians to the Maya*. New York: Simon & Schuster, 2002.

Townsend, Richard F. *The Aztecs*. London: Thames & Hudson, 1992.

Van Tuerenhout, Dirk T. *The Aztecs: New Perspectives*. Santa Barbara, Calif.: ABC-CLIO, 2005.

Index

D H A R M A   A R T

12-20-02   X

DHARMA ART

CHÖGYAM TRUNGPA

EDITED BY JUDITH L. LIEF

SHAMBHALA • *BOSTON & LONDON* • 1996

Shambhala Publications
Horticultural Hall
300 Massachusetts Avenue
Boston, Massachusetts 02115

9 8 7 6 5 4 3 2 1

First Edition

Printed in the United States of America

⊗ This edition is printed on acid-free paper that meets the American National Standards Institute Z39.48 Standard.

Distributed in the United States by Random House, Inc., and in Canada by Random House of Canada Ltd

Library of Congress Cataloging-in-Publication Data

Trungpa, Chogyam, 1939–
    Dharma art/Chögyam Trungpa; edited by Judith L. Lief. — 1st ed.
      p.   cm. — (Dharma ocean series)
    ISBN 1-57062-136-5 (alk. paper)
     1. Buddhism and the arts.   I. Lief, Judith L.   II. Series:
Trungpa, Chogyam, 1939–   Dharma ocean series.
    BQ4570.A72T78   1996   96-14961
    294.3'375—dc20   CIP

D H A R M A   A R T